A
Poetry Archive

Volume 7
Five Seasons 2016 - 2017

Frank Prem

Wild Arancini Press
2025

Publication Details

Title: A Poetry Archive Volume 7
         Five Seasons — 2016 - 2017

ISBN: 978-1-923166-44-8 (p-bk)
ISBN: 978-1-923166-45-5 (e-bk))

Published by Wild Arancini Press
Copyright © 2025 Frank Prem
All rights reserved:

No part of this publication may be reproduced, stored in a retrieval system, or transmitted in any form or by any means, electronic, mechanical, photocopying, recording or otherwise, without prior written permission from the publisher and author.
A catalogue record for this book is available from the National Library of Australia.

Cover Design: Wild Arancini Press

Welcome. Welcome. Welcome the new!

CONTENTS

A Poetry Archive Volume 7: Five Seasons

Introduction 1

    Spring 2016 3

    Summer 2016 141

    Autumn 2017 287

    Winter 2017 385

    Spring 2017 505

After Words 655

    Author Information 657

    Other Published Works 659

    What Readers Say 661

    Index of Poems 665

A Poetry Archive Volume 7: Five Seasons

Introduction

The *A Poetry Archive* series gathers the greater part of Frank Prem's poetic work that has not appeared in dedicated collections elsewhere.

This volume, *A Poetry Archive Volume 7: Five Seasons*, grew out of a *Poem A Day* project that espanned sixteen months. It became an extended practice in sustained attention, daily reflection, and the steady development of voice.

The collection includes a number of small sequences of contemplation, including the *Axeman* series, and marks the first emergence of what has become Prem's personal short-form practice: Seventeen Syllable Poetry.

During this period, Prem also developed an approach to writing that drew upon accompanying images, either to illustrate a poem or to inspire it.

For this printed edition, the images have been removed. Some poems that relied heavily on their visual counterparts have also been omitted. This decision was due to print quality limitations, loss of original images, or because the work stood more strongly without them.

Future volumes in the Archive may include images, and may be produced in colour to support that inclusion.

As always, each poem here is intended to stand as a complete story in itself.

Spring 2016

except the fire

I have muted every sound
bar the crackle
of the fire

the drone of a distant plane . . .

the wind-rush of a car
flying in its glee
down the straight stretch of road
that is the street outside . . .

a murmur —
soft —
from the kitchen fridge
that whispers of chill nothing . . .

should I care to listen

I do not

I am in the silence
of muted sounds

except
the fire

hume dam — away to freedom

*shush rush shush rush
shushashashashusharush
shusharush and shusharush*

I am BOOMING

my passion drives
this river

shusharush and shusharush

I am POURING

brilliant splashing
foams

*shushashashashusharush
shushashashashusharush*

you cannot STOP me

look around
do you see
I am GONE GONE
I am GONE away

shush rush shush rush

watch me flow AWAY AWAY
to freedom

shusharush and shusharush

my water FALLS
to freedom

shushashashashushashah

Spring 2016

three birds: pigeon, magpie, rosella

pigeons
wheeling around

they circle
across a grey sky
bending the air

the flock is *one*
I know

~

magpie
sharpening his beak
on the high branch

every leaf is gone

this place
is exclusive to
the black and white king
now go!

~

rosella red
thinks I don't see her

squabble squawk
pretty thing

you mean no harm
what harm *could* you
from blue

is creating the divine

like a snowflake

captured pure and white

a-gleam
inside a flower

by the sun adored

a plum tree
creates the divine

there - at the gorge

did I once swim
in that sweet pool

where a rose-blush
lies now upon the honey
and laughter
bubbles the white water

under the curtain shelf
of that little waterfall . . .

did I catch
a glimpse of *me* in there
hiding
from you

did you find me

do you still seek among the wilds
of that long forgotten
creek bed

reach out your hand
right now
and I'll be there

for you

still waiting

dancing the fire in the evening

with a flare and a flame
the little piece of pinewood
is on fire

a crackle and a roar
snatch the breath right out
of the air

see the devils dance

> *(dance!)*
> *(dance!)*

turn and tumble
twist in contortions

> *(dance!)*
> *(dance!)*

coal is glowing red
sending ripples
in semaphore

> *(dance!)*
> *(dance!)*

and the devils

> *(dance!)*
> *(dance!)*

yes the devils
the devils are aflame
in this red

> *(dance!)*
> *(dance!)*

Spring 2016

down without care

down come the waters

> *from rock-pool*

> *to shallow*

> *to fall*

> *and*

> *to cascade*

granite is gentled
a-lull
by the stream

yellow and pink
in the sun

but moss must hold
in the absence
of any *where*

its grip clinging
to an *idea*
of anchorage

while down come the waters
from rock-pool to shallow

no care in the world
but cascade

coyote moon

coyote moon
high up in the sky
I raise my head
to salute you

>*oh-oh-oh*

>*o-oh*
>*oh-oh-oh*

cloud in the sky
hides my coyote moon

>*oh-oh-oh*

I raise my head

>*oh-oh-oh-oh*

howling moon

river call to morning

there is a river
running beneath my backyard

channelled into a pipe
under the ground
to take water
from a natural spring
away

down to the gorge
and then the murray river

it runs in a trickle
all through every day

it runs
in a torrent
when it rains

and at night
in my room
when the world outside
is quiet . . .

I hear the waters
of that river
call
like a lullaby
to sweet my sleep

    sleep sleep

calls the river

    drift with me
    as we ride

*from a tiny stream
to the mighty murray*

*sleep
and sleep
till tomorrow morning*

*sleep and sleep
till tomorrow's morning*

a journey of raindrops

when they fall
they begin from the bottom
of the top

> *soaring gliding flying*
> *colliding avoiding riding*

they stop their fall —
a dead halt —
when they strike the top

> *pounding smashing splatting*
> *rebounding soaking landing*

where the earth meets the sky
they journey no more

after storm

beyond the yester-rain
is a mist
that stills the *now*
and constrains the thought
that would be loud
to the merest whisper

a *susser*
with a trailing touch

suggestion
yet not tempest

within the thickened hush
an embodiment of *shiver*
moves a linger
from the storm that was

but the sun will burn

the wisps will rise
and rise
to begin
again

beyond the remnant shiver
begins new day

digestive fibonacci: fractal-izing mandelbrot

there was a slow sliding small snail
in a fibonacci shell
winding its way up a broccoli
that had woven itself
into a mandelbrot

romanesque!

twists and twirls
delved deep enough
to fractal-ise an unwary eye
that gazed too long
or plunged too far

but the snail —
who wound around from the beginning —
kept mathematically safe
and quite secure
for the ratio was golden

> *one mollusc*
> *one brassica*
> *and a bite off the top*

that
is *one-to-one*

perhaps one bite more
would sweeten the numbers . . .

and as it climbed
do you know
I don't think that it really cared

from within the shell
there was just
the journey

the *way*
and the end in sight

a fibonacci-slug
has no need
to understand a mandel-broc
after all
but it digests
what it can while it wanders
round
and around
and around

round
round and around
and around

goodnight, my western sky

every evening the sun
speaks to the western sky

>*goodnight*

>*goodnight dear host*
>*I will leave you*
>*colour*

>*I will paint you red*
>*I will gleam in yellow*
>*I will take the shading away*

>*leave you*
>*brilliant in white*
>*before you fade to sleep*
>*beneath the pinpoint stars*

>*then tomorrow*
>*I will return*

>*tomorrow*
>*will be a day of gold*

>*so until then*
>*goodnight*
>*my dear western sky*

>*look for me to shine*
>*when the morning comes*

>*and the day*
>*is new begun*

Frank Prem

bowing before (my) royalty

I bow before the mailman
I bow down before the mail

I hold something of a reverence —
perhaps just respect —
for what he's got

it could be a packaged sceptre
maybe a signet
or a crown
that bids me bow low
as low as I possibly can

you may say

    eleven cents . . .

    well
    what is all the fuss

or accuse me

    you're overplaying

    this is really
    not that much

but
I bow low
before the mailman
and
(my) royalty

an alchemy

flame
flows like water
from the coal bed
up
to yellow-kiss the baffle

embers glow radiance
like a beating heart . . .

the devil
is alive
and dancing

that wood I hewed

> *my splitter*
> *raised*
> *then brought down*
> *to shatter the rounds*
> *into bites and chips*
> *and slices*

is incarnated
into the short-lived god
of fire

looking up

when he looked up
to the sky
the stars shone

darkness filled spaces
between points
of light

from here —
on the ground —
the next place
seemed so very far

he selected a stone
to throw

to reach the heart
of the moon

and it rose
high
only to turn in the air

fall at his feet

~

>   *inter-stellar travel*
>   *should be driven*
>   *by dreams*
>
>   *imagine!*
>   *how far*
>   *he could go*
>   *fuelled by his desire*
>
>   *his passion*
>
>   *the hope in his heart*
>   *would take him*
>   *past mars . . .*

. . . could take him
away
to the furthest stars

~

when I look up
to the night
I see stars shine

anonsom bul

my ensemble is
the keys beneath my fingers
a backlit screen

a-glow

bits
that flow
just like words
across like paper

together
we are one

together
we chase fireflies
and set those sparks alight

together we are more . . .

much more
than I am

together we *are*

with you
we
just are

torrent and warm

a torrent pours
along the flood path
of *mellish canyon*

and I can hear the wind
cry heartbreak
wail and woe

outside the world is rent

    rain has come

    the tempest blows and storms

while here am I
out of the driving squall
tucked in my bed
and warm

who will leave you clean

I have caused the rain
I have brought
the tempest

I have caused the wind to blow
stray webs and loose threads
before it

listen to the song
the wind is howling

hear the deep
low
rumbled roar

that is me

so patter little raindrops
wave and sway
lithe tree

I am with you
but a short time

I will go
you will be clean

stars in his sleeves

we only saw something
when his sleeve
rode up from his wrist
just a little higher

that's where
the skin of his hand
turned into black-ink night
with stars here and there
that twinkled
like a throw of glitter

when he saw we were watching
he went a little bit red
made a cough and a movement
that ended with him tugging
that sleeve down
a little lower

he smiled at the corner
of his mouth
sort of wry as though to say

> *you caught me out*
> *so I best be leaving*

and he was gone
almost before we noticed

I really don't remember
exactly how he looked
I can't visualise the cut
or how long his hair was

but I recall the way
he wore the stars on his arm
on the night
when the sleeve of his shirt
rode just a little bit higher

the wet september why

there has been rain

all my gullies run

debris on the paths
lies in snakes and swales

and in a minute
or so
there is going to be more

this september
wet days
are becoming the norm

but in my rubber boots
I can make quite a splash

wherever I step . . .

    step
    step

is a watery dance

I can twirl around
with my umbrella open
and unfurled

and everyone knows
it is a wet september

the swales
and the rain . . .

they
are the reasons
why

it waits for me

my day
lies just outside the window
where the plum tree has changed
from white
into green
since last I looked
just yesterday

the parrot calls —
a squeaky voice
painted red and blue —
to tell me
I am required

but . . .

I'm still drinking coffee

I ground and brewed it up myself
and I'm not going to do my day-job
until it's gone

the morning is stark
beneath a grim grey sky
and it will just have to wait
before I join it
where it lies waiting
outside
my kitchen window

lazy moon

lazy low moon
in the eastern sky
are you too heavy
to climb

you're hanging so low —
light full in my face —
you're lazy
there are stars waiting
up high

round as a dollar
big as a balloon
clouds drift right past
beneath you

yes you're one of a kind
bright
but sublime
you make shadows dance and
I've got one here beside me

up on the wall
or a run across the road
there's me
and my shadow
and you

(now get up there)

Spring 2016

coffee café before late shift

coffee café
I've done lunch
I'm just killing time
until my shift starts

>   *big flat white*
>   *how strong is that*
>   *I have to stay wide awake for . . .*

an elderly group of five
is all

>   *smiling choppers*
>   *slick silver hair*
>   *and a perm*
>   *a rouge and an oversize handbag*

>   *delicate*
>   *so slow*
>   *picking paths through the tables*
>   *just in case of a . . .*

it's never too early in a day
or a life
to introduce kids to a fluff *baby-cino*

>   *a small boy has rehearsed*
>   *time and time again*
>   *the way to best wear a milk-moustache*
>   *his small sister though has a better cream curl*
>   *and mum and dad are just so pleased they could . . .*

yes and sometimes
you just want it all
but in a world of mod-cons you can't take it
because . . .

> *there's the chirp of the phone*
> *and a selfie to pose*
> *hardly time to get your spoon*
> *into a hummingbird slice*
> *with such a generous dollop of . . .*

coffee café
I'm just killing time
till my shift is ready
to receive me again but
until that hour

> *there's a man placing an order*
> *he's macedonia or greece*
> *wants a takeaway that's going to*
> *stand his hair up . . .*

Spring 2016

I think a feeling (in words)

the words
from my head
are the absolute truth
but
they're a lie

I know
because I thought them

they are real
and they mean what they say
but
I don't trust them

I don't trust *me*

the feelings
in my heart
are at odds with the words
but I believe in *them*
a little more

they are warmer
than words

the heart goes deeper
than a noun
an adverb
or postulation
any protestation
even when they seem justified

it's so easy
to justify words
but a feeling
is

it just *is*

at least
that's *my* feeling

today the time

the cherry trees
are swollen at the bud

some daffodils
have passed along the whisper

>   *it's time to flower soon*

though the rain outside
is still laced in sleet
and the clouds brood
as they plot a path
across a blustery sky
that continues its dance
with the chill winds
of winter

still
it is time

the magpie woke me
with a song this morning
it was early but daylight
was already in the kitchen
readying the aroma
of fresh coffee

the magpie knew
he carolled

>   *it's time*

spring creek radio

spring creek is hosting
a talk show

it burbles on and on
exactly like on radio

snow melt and heavy rain
are the subject of the day
and just when you think
it's all been said
white water brings down more

the voice is deep
as a basso frog
as splash as a gossip
whisper-borne

and then it's gone
downstream
yester-minute news

say
how about this weather
burble burble

the next show's on

burble

burble

a good season (down at the creek)

every hole is a swimming pool
the wombats are gone
seeking higher real estate

sponge mosses can't hold the water in
they're seeping
sloshed and stoned

a good season

Spring 2016

the beginning of life

go away
don't talk to me
Idon'tthinkthat
I am really alive

don't trouble me
till I wake

go away
grind coffee beans
putthemup
on top of the stove

I'll open my eyes when I hear
the hissing
and the bubbling
start

if you want to be the hero —
my hero —
you better brew them hard

and make it strong
enough
to stir my bones

hello
come talk with me
thisdayisupandI
feel that I am *at-em*
truly I
am *at-em* again

coffee is the start of the world

coffee hiss me into life
on the stove

coffee

coffee

coffee is the way to my soul

now I
am
alive

I feel truly
I am *alive*

finding north

    north-north-north-north   north-north-north-north
    north-north-north-north   north-north-north-north

where will I go
what there to find

how far away it seems

always so far away

    north-north-north-north   north-north-north-north
    north-north-north-north   north-north-north-north

    north
            go north
                    go further north

    north-north-north-north   north-north-north-north
    north-north-north-north   north-north-north-north

will I be cold there
I need the warm

is this for the best

which road is mine

    north-north-north-north   north-north-north-north
    north-north-north-north   north-north-north-north

            go north
                    go further north

    north-north-north-north   north-north-north-north
    north-north-north-north   north-north-north-north

I am lost to myself
I'm searching forward

will this road journey end

will my *one day* ever come

north-north-north-north   north-north-north-north
north-north-north-north   north-north-north-north

    go north
        go further   north

                the way
                lies
                inside your heart

north-north-north-north

    north

shoe dance

once I had a dancing shoe
and I would one-step along
when I wore it

the other one
didn't dance at all
it just stuck out its tongue

and
I deplore it!

how rain starts

as though the thought
had conjured the deed
the first drop fell

soon the metal roof
was performing
the raindrop song

and the sound
had both a beat
and innate rhythms
of a driven downpour

but slowed

and slowed

slowed
so the tune could emerge
in staccato one-beats
and twos

spaced apart

to allow the next thought
to rise between

and call down
crescendo

lotus emergent

the vibrant hues
of a lotus flower
unfurl to fill a page

pastel strokes feed life
to a thirst of paper

and this floral water-bird
has raised an open face
to gaze into the burning eye
from the green
of an altar-throne

there is worship here

lotus to the sun

there is worship here

loving strokes of pastel light
and dark
intensity

enough to show
the heart

woolshed in spring

woolshed you are loud
you SHOUT
like an angry man
drunk
on the mead
of mountain water

I will not close with you
I hold no trust
no good faith
you are a belligerence
held too loosely

a hungry waterfall
you

white-water spume
your testosterone
flings froth into the air
to catch and to coat
anyone

everyone

drag them
down
beneath you

arrogant beast
you wait
you just wait —
as I can wait —
until the summer
takes your spunk away

then I will kick
my feet in your waters
I will cross you with a step
from rock to rock

puny little stream

daily: the splits

there are hard ones
there are soft ones
there are cross-grains
and rotten cores

>   *the splitter bites*
>   *the splitter rings*
>   *the splitter*
>   *shatters eucalypt rounds*
>   *far and wide*

one by one
the blocks are transformed
from backyard eminence
into firewood

I stop to catch a breath
and size the task

>   *the next round . . .*
>
>   *a large one*
>   *or a small*

the next round

>   *should I try that knotted piece*
>   *of grandpa wood that fell*
>   *from white-ants*
>   *chewing a highway to the heart*

this is my mountain
daily
I will climb

best words (repainted)

and I see that I
am like a painter
drawn over
and again
to repeat my theme

a self-portrait
sketched in raindrops
then roughed
afresh and differently

the same

in the night
I hear the wind howl
lonely
it sings the low song
to me

even the sunshine
of morning
that brings the green
to new light
is a reminder that I see this
every day

a rosella bells
a magpie sings
the plover screams aloud
and I am re-made
my image . . .

there

before the sound dies
and

    hoo hoo hoo

is that my n . . .

Spring 2016

> *hoo hoo hoo*

it fills me
and I will draw it
in my best words

using my best words
again
for the coming of the wind

> *I live in the house*
> *of the song*
> *of the wind*
>
> *in darkness the gale*
> *calls*
> *and howls*
>
> *I ride the black night*
> *on the sound*
> *of the wind*
>
> *each cry lifts me*
> *up*
> *and beguiles*
>
> ~
>
> *I spurn my sleep*
> *I am waiting*
> *for the wind*
>
> *she sings me*
> *a storm*
> *lullaby . . .*

three presentations

1

surround yourself in silence

for preference
don something black

stand in the sharpness
of a spotlight

say nothing
until it's right
say nothing until . . .

a few words
just a few words

then . . .

hold again
quite still don't move
until the room is shushed at you

say it again
slowly and clear
say it again

then go

2

put the white-face on
dust talcum into your hair

wear a white sack

stand at the mic
speak monotone —
made up monotone —
before you whistle
at the feedback technology
beside you

turn on the static

turn on distortion

turn on the noise

shh
quiet

stand at the mic
speak in a monotone
refer to yourself
the third person

then
turn on the noise

3

wear the performance *akubra*
and a *driza-bone*
over *moleskins*

and elastic-sided boots
the kind you'd wear
as a swaggie
of the modern day

check you in the mirror
then
on to the stage

> *move around*
> *hold attention*
> *move around*

you can't stand still
while reciting the tale
of *clancy*

the *snowy river*

the throat-cut
from *ironbark*

bow
bow low again
and go

exit stage
right

tweedling october

> *tweedle and tweedle and tweedle*
> *dut dut*
> *tweedle and tweedle and tweedle*
> *dut dut*
> *tweedle and . . .*

I've woken from sleep
with music in my head

some kind of reel

> *. . . and tweedle*
> *dut dut*

it's a happy enough tune

spring-in-step
rather than dirge
but there is no reason

outside is grey rain
for the fourth day running

the slosh
is approaching ankles
on the unwary

but in here

> *tweedle and tweedle and tweedle*

we are writing
we are painting
we are assessing the grey
for its qualities
as a subject for poem or paint

october has begun
as september left off

as life
in an art-scape.

> *dut dut*
> *tweedle and . . .*

Spring 2016

belle and beau

    o

called the wind

    I love to run through your leaves
    to spin them around
    make them shine
    with sunlight

~

    yes

the tree replied

    I feel you
    ripple through my leaves
    I feel my branches join you
    dancing

    and the light
    that the sun sends down
    is a sparkle
    and gleam
    that you set free

    blow through me
    that I might
    sway with you
    I hear your music roar
    as you play your song

~

    bow low
    then
    soar o beauty

*clad
in shimmer gown*

*you
are the belle
my forest belle
and I
your breeze
and beau*

quality light

there's a good light
in beechworth
when the rain's been falling
and the sun goes down
when a beam hits a cloud
as it sleets by in regiments
painted grey

there's a good light
after the storm has passed'
perhaps it's the cleanse
that takes all the blur away
but it's a good light that falls
when the sun picks a point
to highlight
for illumination

it's a good light in beechworth
so hand me down the camera
and filter the right lens
for a good light on a rainbow
dressed only in amber
and yellow
from the sun
after the rain
before the night takes a hold
on spring creek

low hanging

the wind is gone

the leaves hang
still

listless

no sun to gleam them
no shine or glisten

but the rain has come
to thunder down
its fall a bitter laughter

the sweet caress
of yesterday
barely stirs
beneath
low-hung branches

rising above ground

> *look*
> *we're flying!*

look
they are flying

with one arm each
clasped about the other's waist
and the other arm waving
a soiled white wing
they have risen
toes off the ground

> *flying!*

so good for them
this experience of flight
and lightness enough
to hover so

they seem so delighted

> *hey*
> *we're really flying!*

and as for me
well
it seems I must grow my feathers
anew
for I miss soaring
on the light
of stars

> *whee!*
> *this is flying!*

the old man's pigeons

he said

> you know
> my breeding pair is getting older
>
> not so long ago
> they'd be in the nest
> at six weeks
> to the day
> and the last lot of chicks
> would get the cold shoulder
>
> now
> they're not so regular
> anymore
>
> sometimes
> there'll only be one egg
> and not a pair
>
> but oh
> they're such pretty birds
> and I watch them
>
> I could get lost
> in the brilliance
> of their snowy white
> soft down
>
> they have nothing in their enclosure
> to make a nest out of
> so I keep bucket beside me
> when I prune the fruit trees
> or clean the yard
>
> small twigs
> little branches
> drifting straw

Spring 2016

I cut them to a good size
for birds
then scatter a handful
across the floor I paved for them

so much joy
for me
when they gather
and build

whatever I throw
however much there is
every last twig
every straw
gets transformed into a home
for snowy down
and ugly chicks
with beaks too large for their heads
and goose bump tufts
all over their skin

my birds
you know
are getting older now

I don't think I'll have them
much longer

on the wind

here I call

in the absence of the wind
from deep within
I send my voice
to you

hear me call

I burst my heart to send
to you
the voice that I can feel
within
in the absence of the wind

I hear you call

with the return of the wind
speaking deep inside
with your voice
is you

here you call me

almost bursting
into my heart
it's your voice that I can feel
inside
at the returning of the wind

here we are
calling

responding
on the wind that blows
between us now
calling
responding
on the wind

here

here
the voice that's in my head
is the sound of the creek
swollen to white water
pushing pushing
rushing rushing

a roar

here
the flash that struck my eye
is the shine of the sun
sliding down the rock face
as water
on granite
and the moment of joy
is the butterflies
gambolling
over and over

around me
as though I were nothing
of note

just another part of the day
like the meltwater sound
of springtime

here

stealing the soul (just a little bit)

once upon a time
some believed that a photograph
was a doorway
into the soul

>*take a picture*
>*take a snap*
>*take a piece of me away*
>
>*keep it behind glass*
>*inside a frame*

and here I am today
taking photographs
here I am today
catching souls

little flower here
little orchid
there

faint pink
in a swatch of heath
and here
I've caught three fungi

these flowers
are the heart of spring
in this gorge land

these waters swirl
with a bursting élan
that feels alive

and
I have it here —
box brownie boy —
I have the soul
to keep
for my own

tree poem

tomorrow
it might be just a wooded arrangement
set there in the yard
for the purpose of holding leaves
supporting birds
swaying a little
when the wind blows hard enough
to move it

tomorrow
it could be an object
of size and girth
that obstructs my lawn mower
forcing me
to go around it

and tomorrow after
it will be sitting
on the boundary
saying
doing nothing
beyond biding time
while the seasons pass
as they surely will

but today I see
a magnificence
perfectly framed by a rectangle
formed by the back door

I see a straight spine
reaching for the sky
holding branches outstretched
like an offering of benediction
and birds
squeaking and dancing
across those boughs

tree

> *grand master*
> *majesty*

tree

> *high riser*
> *oh what a glorious*

tree

> *today I'm in awe of what I have*
> *right here before me*
> *tree*

too cool for (magpie) school

sharp black
sharp white
sharp beak
all right
sharp magpie

this magpie is too cool
for school

approaching a small mountain
of mulch
it is important
to maintain an appearance
of control
while strolling up the hillside

the feet
however
are down below
and out of sight

so it's a
shuffle-dance-shuffle
with one foot
to find firm balance
while attempting nonchalant

    peck

    peck

and another
dance-dance two-step
followed by
no-no-no definitely not
a stumble

three paces backwards

peck

peck

this mound of dirt
is not worth it
ma-an

there's better strutting
on new-cut lawn
for a dude
who's so

sharp

a husqy roar

I am the grass cutter
nothing is going to stand
in my way

I'll jump aboard
the ride-on mower and drive

cruise up to the back fence
cut a straight un-deviated line
swing it wide to the right
then turn down

hustle hustle run
it's been sunny
but on a mowing day
there's every chance it could rain

so here I fly
at five miles an hour
listen to my husky roaring
like a bladed demon

and my grass is lawn again
beautiful and green
except for the soggy bit

the rough and rocky bit

and that part there
where I smote the fence
with my bull bar

yes
yes
I'm the grass cutter

listen to my husky roar

I love
my
husqy!

a little light (darker)

what do I know about
this world I'm in

I know
that it has to be saved

and I know that
once upon an idyll time
it was a garden
but
the garden is gone

what do I know about
growing things

I know
that we've forgotten the way

and I know that
instead of food
in our gardens
we'd rather we ate
our own young
who'd rather they ate us
entire

what do I know about
gardens

I know
I need soil on my hands

and I know that
I need to plant harmony
around every compass point
and every small place
that I glance

Spring 2016

I know you'll read this
as a strange piece of work
the writing seems
a little
awry
but a good voice has died
and when I look outside
today

it seems
just a little light
darker

imagination (patter pitter)

I heard a drop of my imagination fall
and touch down
gentle
on the roof outside

it brought a friend
or maybe more
to set up a slow percussion

> *patter patter*
>
> *patter pitter patter*
>
> *they danced*

I looked outside
to watch the rain descend
to see the drops as each one fell

there was nothing in the sky above
but clouds swirling
in slate and grey

> *misty twirls*
>
> *smoke ghost curls*
>
> *they danced*

I heard my imagination fall
in a patter in a swirl
in a misty rain it fell

and it danced
on the roof
danced in the sky
danced in my mind

Spring 2016

pitter patter pitter
was the rhythm
so

even if there's rain
on the roof outside
there is dance

yes
even in the rain
we can dance

for a magpie

magpie
that beak is sharp already

there's no need
to keep on honing

magpie
preen it through your feathers

black and white
in monochrome

magpie
go stalking with a sharp spear

those worms
are yours alone

then magpie
sing me a fine song

magpie
let's sing it in duet

magpie
you start and I
will sing right along

magpie
together better yet

>   *singing magpie*

>   *sharpened beak*

>   *preening feathers*

>   *worms to feast*

just for a magpie

Spring 2016

ready for a feed (baby magpie)

hungry

    I'm so hungry

I could eat my mother

    so hungry

I could eat my father

    I'm hungry

I could eat this garden pole

    hungry

I could eat a buttercup

    so hungry

I'll try to eat a blade of grass

    I'm hungry

ack ack ack ack

    hungry

mama

    so hungry

papa

    I'm hungry

I could eat *me* in this window

    hungry

I really look quite tasty

    so hungry

I want to eat me *now*

    I'm hungry

mum,
where's my tucker
because I
am very hungry

reducing the rounds

two rounds of wood
one atop the other

one is *the smiting block*
the other
is pieces of firewood
in potentia

and *I* . . .

I am *the splitter*

holding that implement
in my hand
hefting the weight
to obtain the balance
in the sweet spot
where *it* is me and I am
the splitter

working around the perimeter
slicing the round into pieces
to be mounded
while I swing

while I smite

there's nothing so sweet
as the sound of my edge
biting deep

creating a fissure

to strike
and to strike
until the monster round
is reduced . . .

reduced again

nothing left
to challenge my firebox

stack it away
under cover
let it dry and wait
the other end of summer

bakery sparrow

the bakery sparrow
does not wear the apron
of a baker

and he does not put his money down
to buy a *flat white*
or a *latte*
and a sweet bun

he doesn't wield a mop

doesn't
serve at table
nor does he exchange
small nothings
over a morning tea slice
of biscuit or cake

he plays no banjo
on a sunday morning
for the tourist trade

but he hops and he bounces
from the ground
up onto a table

takes the crumbs
that have been left
behind

and he chirps to his friends
that he has found

> *good pickings*
> *good breakfast*

they join him
his brothers and his sisters
there can be no doubt

this
is a good time

the bakery sparrow takes a moment
to fluff
and shake his tail

it's been an excellent morning
everybody has been fed
and they are happy
so . . .

it is time —
under the middle morning sun —
to go home

tenderfoot dancer

well
he took off his shirt
then he plucked a hairy weed
out of the lettuce bed

dropped his blue-jeans
and stepped out of the leggings
by the broccoli

cast his vest away to one side
before he leaned down
to check the snow peas out

to assess the way
the beans
have grown

his short shorts were no use
so they flew
right across
two potato hills

but he retained his old hat
because the sun was out

and he danced some kind of
rain-come-hither
every time he put his foot down
on a stick
or on a stone

he wondered

> *is it really naked gardening*
> *the way they describe it in my book*
> *if I keep*
> *my wide-brim on . . .*
>
> *to keep the sun away*

he didn't know

but he was trying
his best

> *tenderfoot planting*
> *tenderfoot dancing*

naked gardening

a good girl

>*erf erf*
>*erf erf*
>
>*erf erf*
>*erf erf*

it's always the same

when joe goes out
to *rotary*

>*erf erf*
>*erf erf*
>
>*erf erf*
>*erf erf*

when he's working on the engine
with *the old cranks club*

>*erf erf*
>*erf erf*

roxie is at home

>*erf erf*
>*erf erf*

all alone

when joe goes
out for a small drink
down to the pub
every friday night

>*erf erf*
>*erf erf*

roxie spends the night alone
calling out
to him

> *erf erf*
> *erf erf*

calling out
joe come home

she's calling out *joe*
won't you please come home

> *erf erf*
> *erf erf*

all night long

> *erf erf*
> *erf erf*

till the moment joe
walks in the door

> *erf erf*
> *erf erf*

to pat her on the head

> *erf erf*
> *erf erf*

tell her
what a good girl
she's been

all alone at home

erf erf
erf erf

what a very good girl
she has been

such a good dog

axeman: oh fiddleback

>
> *one chop*
>
> *two chop*

now
there's supposed to be
more firewood
less round

> *one chop*
>
> *two chop more*

I have creased the round
at four points now
but nothing is changed

> *one chop*
>
> *two chop*
>
> *one chop*
>
> *two chop*

it's a gnarly old mongrel
that won't even give up
its splinters

twisty twisty
bendy arc
of snaking fiddleback

> *one chop*

my woodpile!

> *just chop*

Spring 2016

stop counting

chop

chop

yes it fell

the silky oak fell
when nobody heard it falling

I know it happened
because it is lying there
on the ground

the man next door
came home from melbourne
and brought a chainsaw

every branch and bough
made smoke on an outside pyre

and what of the local magpies
who come at the end of their day
they loved that tree
like home

every evening
around sundown
up around the highest leaves
one would sit in silhouette
like a sentinel

and the starlings' vulgar chatter
never will be heard again
they'll need to move their dorm
to an oak tree

yes
I know the silky oak fell
though no one heard it go
I know that it fell
by the absence
of the magpies

a coffee song

it's time to play
the coffee song
grind it right up
put it on
stove radio

it's a quiet start
I'd hardly even know it was there
but the element is glowing
so something's going on
down below

and in the distance
far away
like the growl of thunder
the sound of pressure
building in a confined space
lodges in the front of my brain

I start to bop
without my own volition
while I watch the milk
rise to the boil

it's less a sound
more a feeling
as the steam percolates
and the beans express themselves
through the water

to rise again
as a different being
with a rumble and a roar
like the diesel of a coffee train
crashing around the kitchen

steam
screams out to me

come and pour

right now
right now
right now

this is a coffee song

I sing it out loud
every
coffee morning

ride the portent

here am I
flying on the portent of a storm

clouds roll by

they brush my hair
a tousle in affection
then they go

and thunder rumbles
threatening
behind me

a laggard
but I know
it will not stop chasing

lightning makes the horizon-line
shine brightly
then strobe
in an instant back to dark

flash
and crash
and roar
a light and sound crescendo

with the rain
pell-mell helter-skelter
sideways
pelting a fury
as it falls

I ride

I
am the portent
of a storm

the wind at war

the wind and the tree fought
a battle last night

usually
skirmishes blow up
shake some branches
then pause
as a truce is struck

but this time
the siege won out

for weeks there was rain
brought by the wind
to weaken resistance

the tree held its ground
shed a few leaves
defiant
resistant
un-swaying

then sometime after dark
a new legion of rain soldiers
was brought by the wind
to determine the outcome

today
there's a large tree down
the battle is done

the wind has moved on
to seek terms
with a forest

the lingering breeze
kisses the last seed
carries it off like a promise
to rest in a place
where new peace lies

dissatisfiction

every book I hold
I feel I've read before

there's nothing new in fantasy
since frodo
came back home

murder crimes are all too
by-the-numbers

your suspenseful thriller . . .

a penny
will fetch a dozen

good space opera
it seems
only happens
stars and worlds
away

when all I want —
my small wish —
is to hold a good book
in my hands

something where
I can be grabbed
and held
by the opening lines

a hero's tale
or a mystery
that is a joy
to try to work out

but my local library is full of tomes
when what I want
is to hug to my chest
an adventure
on every page

I guess it's back
to mordor for me
yet again

alone (with the wind)

empty house

I
am all alone

there is no sound
except my heartbeat
and an echo of *woo-woo* wind

this house
is a playground
for the curly breezes
sweeping the veranda
fluting the chimney

    ooo
    woo-woo-woo

even my thoughts sing

    ooo
    woo-woo-woo

and now
and now the rain
fingers shushing
a crepe
diminuendo

shhh

see the tree wave its leaves
outside

    ooo
    woo-woo-woo

all alone

we are alone

shhh

    ooo
    woo-woo

the wind and I

    ooo

secrets of the sough

whispered
by a soughing breeze
to ears of grass
that stood so tall

now
burden bowed
their heads nod down
lowered
towards the ground

how they wish —
now it has passed —
they had never heard
the secrets
of the sough

a wake in lockington

in lockington
the water is deep and brown
the canal sort of
meanders through

vermillion and white
the lilies smile
above their mud-stained
lily pads

there is purple
blue grass
and the gazanias
are wild

a riot in the near-side
five acres

the duck does not like me

she is teal

in the sun
the canal runs south
while she flies north
and I am left standing

to watch the wake
go by

bird on the menu

the short-sighted scholar
sat to chicken dinner one night
all the while
intensely pontificating

when dinner was served
so taken was he
by his fantastic thought
that he chewed up the menu

ignored
the roast bird

claiming credit

the water is *on*
like rain falling down
but
I control it
with a turn of the tap

this is *spigot love*
for the vegetables
that are supposed
to be growing

but who knows
the state of the game
when the garlic has gone
to flower
and the silver beet
has had enough
of this place
and started reaching
for the sky

I really had great hopes
you know
for root vegetables
like the carrots
and the hollow crown parsnips

but they have dragged their tails
have not really risen
above dirt height
and I think I might need
to start them
over again

maybe I will do better
with a passionfruit
on the back fence-line

Spring 2016

I don't know
but . . .

it is a good thing —
perennial —
starts over again
without me
while I watch
and claim
it is *my* doing

birthday surprise (an occasion unravelling)

birthday morning

café cooked breakfast

juice
then coffee

the paper

~

eggs fried
mushrooms
bacon on toast
with spinach

ah
spinach

but wait . . .

is that . . .

it looks to be
a hair

a string

something curly

between fingers
he pulls the culprit away
from the bacon
from beneath the toast

and he tugs it
a little more

and then more

and then more

Spring 2016

two hands now
this is surely
some conjurers trick
played especially for the occasion

for the curly hair —
or facsimile of same —
is still emerging
as he hauls now
with vigour
and drags it away
from beneath the innocent
innocuous
toast slice

as time passes
small by small
beside the table
a hair-mound grows
tugged and extracted
without relent

he looks around the café
as this extraordinary thing
is drawn from his left
to accumulate
beside his right

and he glimpses
as he glances
the waitress
in mid-collapse
behind the counter

she seems to shrink
falling inward
then disappears

leaving only a soft-uttered
oh
behind her

and a small —
hardly heard —
whisper
in appeal for

    help

not (at all)

there is a bottle of red —
slowly diminishing —
and me

I'm contemplating

> *what is a thought*
> *what is today*
> *what is the way I need*
> *to marry the two*
> *together*

there's no answer
until I look back

there it is . . .

in the first verse
the second stanza

the third line

there it is

~

this is the fourth time
just today
that I have made a start

but none would roll right
out of my head
off my tongue
onto a new page
the way that they ought to

and I have a lined pad
full of scrawls
full of swirls

full of my idle moments
and half ideas
half wrote-downs

a third of almost
almosts

almost

I look back
I can't read it
can't decipher

>   *where was it*
>
>   *where was my head that time*
>
>   *what was I thinking*
>
>   *who was the man*
>   *that wrote that down*
>
>   *was he*
>   *serious*
>
>   *really serious*

oh well
I don't know
today

this
is today

this is
the best that I've got
and
not much —
not really much —
to offer you
at all

stilling wrath on the horizon

the wrath of gods
is strewn across the sky
in ropes of cloud
painted red
and orange
and purple

as though it is on fire

and I watch
as the blue of day
becomes a kaleidoscope
becomes a rainbow
in full broil

the cosmic soup has been stirred
from somewhere above
and well beyond

I can't stop watching it
the play
as colours hue
from golden white
to shades
you do not see
other places

only there
in the western sky
beyond the day
just at the place
where night falls

and the wrath of gods
is cooled
by descending dark
and event lighting

timed to fade
with the kiss *goodbye*
of today's angry sun

the horizon
has all the colour life
that was ever made
for this world

hammer love

the hammer swings

sharp
metal kiss

hard and blunt
the smiter

the anvil weeps
but . . .

a kiss
is a kiss

woe comes
when a caress
speaks its heart
in such an ungentleness
of touch

yes
there is sorrow —
enough for all of us —
in this love

the old pen

old pen . . .

my old friend

blue
in swirls
and
the rambling scrawl
of thoughts
pinned on to paper

old pen . . .

away when

you wrote my ideas
in stories
start
and middle
and end

old pen . . .

dear friend

thank you
for the poems

for the dreams we caught
together

my
old pen

Spring 2016

tidying up the kitchen migraine

mid-throb

I reached
to get the butter

mid-throb

I held it in my hand
turned —
smooth —
to the fridge
and replaced it

mid-throb

the salt
looks just like
the butter should

mid-throb

there is pepper
and there is yellow
in a tub

mid-throb

how did the shaker of *iodised*
land inside the fridge . . .

I just don't know

mid-throb

some days it's hard
to make
good kitchen sense

mid-throb

mid-throb

put the tea-towel
in the sink
and get some suds in

might as well . . .

mid-throb

get the breakfast washing-up
out of the road

mid-throb

why is there coffee liquid . . .

mid-throb

in a cup
at the bottom
of my washing up sink
with a tea-towel
and bubbling brown suds

and oh . . .

mid-throb

the kettle is filled
with fresh-boiled water

mid-throb

perhaps I should
make that cup . . .

Spring 2016

mid-throb

of cha

or did I already
do that once
today

mid-throb

mid-throb

where did I put
the tea towel

bones (just bones)

I saw
the hand coming up

I saw
the fingers

twisted out of shape
and grasping as they rose

> *grasp to catch something*
> *unawares*

~

I saw
the smile shining on a skull

and I saw the rictus

happy happy joy
just to be out of the grave

> *teeth and jaws*
> *clickety clacky gigglers*

~

I saw
a skeleton at dance

I saw it limbo

nothing goes low
like a bunch of bendy bones

> *play xylophone*
> *on that rib cage*

~

I saw the hand
one dark dark night

I saw
the hand
and then I saw
the fingers . . .

conditional garden

rain is falling
on my seed bed

I watch
to see tomatoes rise
there is no peace
for me
in the garden

I watch to see them
rise

>   *is it an act of love
>   to put the seeds in*

>   *is it love
>   to give a start*

>   *is it love to wait
>   tormented
>   to see which of them
>   will rise*

I am not
an unconditional gardener

I expect
something
in return

but I cannot hold back
the hand that grasps
the seed pack

>   *in they go
>   too early*

>   *in they go
>   too late*

there is nothing
quite like
nothing
so I plant
to fill the spaces

yes
I plant
to fill the spaces
of my quite conditional
garden

axeman: axe bound

I bind myself
within the axe
become the sharp steel
driving

cleave the wood —
a full cord of it
maybe more —
at my feet

the shattered
lie fallen

round on round
mounts my splitting block
round on round
I dispatch them

> *I am the troubling knife*
> *I the axe*
> *I the blade*

trouble I pledge
for this wood
in its rounds

> *I am the promise*
> *bound*

wattlebird sprinkle

the wattlebird
is whipping his caruncles around

making a fan
with his tail as he flies
through the spray
of my sprinkler

the summer has come
all of twelve days
early
and it is as hot as I prefer it to be
much later
in the season

while my sprinkler
is early-saving the vegetables
wattlebird
is diving
like a dancer

> *water my wing tips*
> *water my*
> *underside*
> *water my tail feathers*
> *when I lift them*

wattlebird
wattlebird
summer comes

and we are dry
already

somewhere else

a baby magpie
is confused

more grey than black
a juvenile stub
for a beak

he has encountered
a pane of glass
leaned at an angle
to the plant box

beyond the pane
is a succulent
morsel

at first
he is content
to explore
by lowering his head

reaching
underneath
the edge of the glass

then
a peck
aimed directly at the morsel
through the glass

no

a step backward
brings new perspective

suddenly

there is another magpie
in the glass

Spring 2016

a stumble
an ungainly roll

a shake of the head

a ruffle
of feathers

and another morsel beckons

elsewhere

rough love

suddenly
the sun comes
burning down

suddenly
it is summer

the mystery of a cloud
has disappeared
inside itself

the wonder of rain
turned into a question

I can see the breeze
is still moving leaves

I see them shiver
as it rustles them
blowing by

but there is no breathy kiss
for me

not from the wind

no kiss for me

not from the rain

just a violent grasp
from a roughshod lover
a violent sear
from the sun

a baking bed
and heat

oh
I can't bear it

Spring 2016

he keeps me
too close

he holds me
too long

he is rough love

my sun comes
only to burn me

tarn-tarn OOF! – a rain dance

>*tarn-tarn-ta-ta-ta-tarn-tarn* OOF! OOF!

>*tarn-tarn-ta-ta-ta-tarn-tarn* OOF! OOF!

I am stamping around the kitchen
to a little . . .

I don't know . . .

maybe a classical
beat

>*ta-ta ta-tarn-tarn* OOF! OOF!

I don't usually do this

at least
not always

>OOF! OOF

it's just that

there's this tiny wee drop
of constipated rain
that's attempting to fall

and
I'm trying to get a good beat

a strong rhythm
going
as an encouragement

with sound effects

>OOF! OOF *ta-ta ta-tarn-tarn*

on the OOF!

who knows
it may help and anyway . . .

where's the harm in a little

    ta-ta ta-tarn-tarn

how can that hurt

    OOF!

climbers rescued

the moon is big
and round
tonight

something calls me
to her

I've never seen her
come so close

so near

~

if I grasp the rope
with both my feet
wrap one arm around it . . .

perhaps
I can reach up
to caress her
with the other

~

>*luna*
>*you seem so pale*
>*you are soft and golden*
>
>*luna*
>*have you come so close*
>*for me*
>*his time*

~

the moon is big
and round
tonight

Spring 2016

I've been climbing
to get closer

watching her
it's like she smiles
for me

she waits
~

> *oh luna*
> *now you've gone*
> *so far away*
> *though I have not yet*
> *reached you*
>
> *luna*
> *was I too slow*
> *were you*
> *dismayed*

~

I took too long

I didn't try
quite hard enough

I took the wrong way
to try to reach her

she is gone

gone
beyond my reach
and I
am
lost

alone
on this wretched hill
mount tibrogargan

with ghosts

I went to sleep
with ghosts last night

some dead
some still living

>*conundra*

whispered softly

the *why*
and *what*
of long ago
anew as though
right now
again

again

in my mind
they whirl around
spinning like a dervish

fling them

>*one*
>*another*
>*all the rest*

away
that I might be
in peace

some little peace
until
my spectres all
return

job of the day

yesterday
the task was rain

to hear it fall
hard

enough to rattle iron

from staccato
tapping
becoming solid
until it filled the air
with sound

inspiring the magpie
to become
a chortling accompanist

~

today
the task is golden light

a green
in the trees

blueing the above
until it feels
like home

and it is the blackbird
solo
who sets the tone
bright
reverberating

~

each day
has it's own job
to be performed

Frank Prem

a casual meeting with the banjo

https://frogs.org.au/frogs/species/Limnodynastes/dumerili/

well hello
mister pobblebonk
it's long-time-no-see
my friend

fancy finding you
just here
where I am working

> *with my shovel*
>
> *with my fork*
>
> *with a heavy hammer*

but
do not be concerned
I see you there
and all is well

tell me
have you just woken
from a long sleep

winter was very hard
this year

are you out now
searching
for a nice feed

or
maybe a love match
to meet down the swamp
this evening

could romance
be in store . . .

well in that case
I better rosin the strings
on my fiddle
and you better get your banjo
and the picks
then we'll sing a little
together

> *pobblebonk*
> *pobble-*
> *bonk*

a little song

> *pobblebonk*
> *pobble-*
> *bonk*

it's a very little tune
but it has a rousing chorus
I'll sing it with you
while we both play

something like this

> *pobble*
>
> *pobble*
> *pobble*
> *pobblebonk*

again

> *pobble*
>
> *pobble*
> *pobble*
> *pobblebonk*

yes
that's the way it goes

>   *pobble*

>   *pobble*
>   *pobble*

Spring 2016

my a*** belongs to the government

I'm not
in any way
paranoid

no
I'm not

but I believe
the government
is after my arse

~

the day that I turned fifty —
it was quite a long time
ago —

the government
sent me a letter
signed
with love

> *send us*
> *a little specimen*

they asked

> *collect it*
> *on a stick*
> *that we'll provide*

> *it's for your own good*

> *trust us*

> *we love you have you very best*
> *interests*
> *in mind*

~

well I ignored that letter
as you can
well believe

no specimen of mine
is going
for tests in some
white coated
lab

no thank you

~

today
I was anxiously
awaiting

the mail should bring
an exciting new
old tome

>   *I bought it on e-bay*
>
>   *a french philosophy*
>
>   *a book that's going to set*
>   *my poetic heart*
>   *on fire*

and there
when I glanced out
of my window

a package
too big to fit inside
my little mailbox

>   *oh boy*
>
>   *oh boy oh boy*

~

Spring 2016

*hello frank
this
is your government*

*last chance now
we're asking you nice
we're asking kindly*

*where
is your specimen*

*don't try to tell us
that collecting it
was too hard*

*we gave you
the spoon
we gave
the jar*

*we gave a stamped-return-envelope
and each step
illustrated
on a how-to-do card*

*we want our your specimen
we want it now*

*we need to
take deep look
inside your bowels*

why do you resist us

we are your friends

*if you don't return this
the friendship ends
takes on a new twist*

*your specimen
NOW*

*we await
your swift reply*

the last annual show

wandering around
the annual show
I see the same names
winning every prize

in the bonsai
the succulents
the red roses

in the preserved fruits
in the handcrafts
and fancy stitching

neil says

> *sure*
> *you can take*
> *my picture*
>
> *because I've won*
> *half the show*
> *with exhibits of my own*
>
> *I'm everywhere*
> *but*
> *this could be the last year*
>
> *because everyone is tired*
> *and they don't want to organize*
> *anymore*
>
> *see the committee*
> *is hovering*
> *around eighty*
>
> *none of them can compute*
> *except to skype*
> *with their great grandchild*

*so they want to keep everything
by pen
and by paper*

*but in a digital age
even the fruit preserves
demand a little more*

*and no one
wants to put their hand up
for volunteering*

*and nobody wants
to take time out
from facebook
twitter
and things like that*

*so this show
might be the last one
that you can come to*

*you better catch
a carny ride
because they won't be back*

*and my bonsai
well
I'll still trim it
(that one's a moreton bay fig)
and I couldn't quit this
if I tried*

but I won't be back

*there's no place
for old crafts
or
slow growing
anymore*

the crocodile trainer

I am the crocodile trainer

I have a plastic egg-flip
in my hand
and six sets of teeth
are smiling up at me
as I line them up

side-by-side

big one on the left
descending in size
to the
big one on the right
who's now climbing
all over his neighbour

> *hey! hey!*
> *watch out for my sheets*
> *with those claws*
>
> *tonight I have to sleep*
> *in that*
> *again*

I have delivered a smack
sharp across the tip
of a nose

and somehow my egg-flip
seems to get
a good response

and there they are . . .

my croco-stars

six mouths open

*six in a simultaneous
hiss*

and I am ready
to wake up now

job done

the crocodile-trainer's job
is done

venus of the eucalypts

the grey queen
dances

arms raised
head laid back
and high up in the clouds

her body sways

her hair hangs
down

naked
she is smoothest skin
smoothest silk
to touch

the wind breathes

sighs

and she laughs
a little

    sha sha

a little

    sha sha sha

grey queen
dancing

Spring 2016

last one

today
is the last day
of november

it's a hot one

I can't wait
to get myself to the pub
to buy a beer

to buy another

I don't drink so often
that it ever gets old
but today
is the last day

I've been working
since way before
the sun got warm

I haven't had a chance
to take my pen
into my hand
and I'm due one more
before that sun goes down
so here it is

here
is the last

the final one
I've written down
for november

and that
my friends
is the last I will do
for Spring

Summer 2016

Summer 2016

like summer (to me)

>   *the first cicada*
>   *flew today*

I can hear it singing
tonight

>   *a possum leapt*
>   *right across my head*
>   *to feed in the loquat tree*

>   *a parrot*
>   *in its finery*
>   *shone green*
>   *and blue and red*

>   *then landed soft*
>   *amid a branch*
>   *of red cherries*

that feels
like summer
to me

>   *a koala is grunting*
>   *in a tree*
>   *across the street*

>   *and the fox*
>   *with her cubs*
>   *are at play on a lawn*

and that feels —
pretty much —
like summer
to me

chopping a cord

it has turned into
a summer job

I have dawdled
for too long

by now I should have
chopped my way
through next winter

but the heat
has caught me
and now I sweat and toil
on summered days

these rounds of wood
are patient
but they nag

and so
the splitter rises
and so
I hurl myself
into this work
of seperating cellulose
and lignin

my sweat —
the only moisture
I can see —
is falling
from the precipice
of my nose

~

how big
is a cord of wood

Summer 2016

> *it's bigger*
> *than this*

how long will it take
to chop one cord

> *a lot longer*

when can I stop
to take a drink of water

> *you haven't cut*
> *your cord yet*
> *to fuel the fire*

but
how big
is a cord of wood

> *it's much bigger*

> *keep chopping*

> *keep on*
> *chopping*

climbing

oh lord
how she climbs

reaching up
to the blue world
of the sky
and the evening sun

down here
is green and brown
of dirt
and of the grass

up high
the clouds streak
free to fly along

birds come down
to take their rest
and to chatter
of where they've flown

she listens
she hears them
and lord

how she climbs

Summer 2016

word is to image (in a letter)

sometimes I find that words drag on a lit . . .

regrettably
before he was able
to complete his sentence
on the page
drastic measures became necessary

some time previously
he had acquired —
for this very purpose —
a small wooden mallet

a gavel
of sorts

he gripped it firmly now
raised it
and with a resounding
THUMP
brought it down

on a nascent black and white
grey-smoke creature
attempting to rise
through a squashing
and shaping
of the incomplete sentence

this tendency
for words to free-associate
into unplanned imagery
while he wrote
was increasingly
becoming annoying

Apologies for that mess on the page. It became necessary to crack down on a random phrase that I had not intended. I am wondering if I should change pens, or perhaps revert to a pencil.

If I'm not careful, a word like that can begin to smoke before I've realized and then I end up feeling a little light headed . . .

oh dear
another one

the outline of a man's features —
forehead
eyes
nose
chin
hair and cranium —
had begun to accrete

lit from behind
in a kind of shadow
illumination

THWACK

I'm sorry. My concentration is not what it should be today. I'll have to try to write to you again, tomorrow. I might just as well play a few word games to amuse myself, rather than attempt any serious undertaking.

Regar . . .

almost . . .

almost he had missed
the beginning of an emergence
shaped as a coffin

sigh

THUNK

might as well
enjoy himself
with a little play

    belong

SPLAT

    the extended head
    of an apis mellifera

    passionfruit . . .

SWAT
WHACK

eeuw

that was too much
too graphic

choosing his words
carefully
he placed his pen
on the desk
and turned
his mind
off

old birds refrained

    that one

he said

    you have to be good
    to see that one

we are talking
about a bird
singing

I say
that it's just a blackbird . . .

    no no
    that one
    is not a blackbird

    that one
    is up there
    in the gum tree
    and it sings its heart out
    every afternoon

    I haven't seen it
    (you'd have to be good
    to see it)
    but it isn't
    a blackbird

I've come
for a routine visit

and found them
seated at the table
outside their back door
under the veranda

they're both a bit buggered
today

he can't get enough
air
to allow him to walk
and work

she
has pain in her lower back
that won't let her
straighten up

he still has a twinkle
in his eye
as he argues the merits
of a bird's song

she wears
a long look
as she misidentifies
a magpie
as a currawong

>   *they always come around*
>   *and start singing*
>   *when it's going to rain*

she says it aloud
but no-one really listens

the song
of that bird
is an old refrain

the last red delights

you can hold
the ladder
and a bucket

I'll climb up
on an angle
then reach deep
inside the foliage
to pick
the few ripe cherries
that are almost beyond
my over-balanced reach

but they're
our red cherries
they don't belong
to ratbag parrots

or wattlebirds

and you and I
have had a few
low-hangers
but we've missed out
on the many

so these last tasty treats —
unbalanced
though they may be —
are destined to end up
in our pail

then . . .

let's go eat them

the juice
running down our chins

and
let's go eat them . . .

the tang released
inside our mouths

these cherries
are red delights

these cherries
are the taste of art
inside a small ball package

so
let's go
eat them

seasonal

every year
at about this time
one of them would go
in silent accord
to the cupboard under the stairs
where the old sports gear
boxes of toys
decorations
and sundries resided

a few objects moved
a little space made
until the box was found

snug
among the festive decorations

out it would come
to be dusted clean
and placed with care
and due respect
on the small table
in the lounge

with a little ceremonial flourish
both of them
gathered close –
as participants and spectators –
as the lid
came off

a carefully folded
small package of fur
was delicately removed
and straightened

a button found
and activated
to self-inflate

it made a small
pop
when it was done
and the sound of air moving
faded
then ceased

all that was left to do —
in a ritual
developed between them
over many seasons —
was to rub
and to gentle the ears
between their fingers

softly
a sound became audible
then louder
and unmistakable

    purring

patting
stroking
soft words of endearment
and encouragement

the seasonal cat
opened her eyes
and meowed

oh
the joy

happy hours
of stroking
of rubbing up against people
furniture
legs

then finally
a change

a look in the feline eyes
that was somehow . . .

different

    focused

    hungry

again together
they opened the door outside
and led the way
to the laden trees

cherries
fat baubles of promise
and glow

of juice
and joy
so nearly ripe enough
for the taking

so clearly
already being taken

for there —
plumped as though
in nests of their own making —
were a bower bird
and a parrot

the cat hardly glanced at them
she *knew*

with a leap
she was astride the main trunk
of the first
ornamented tree

with another
she was near to the top

a squawking

a flutter

a small chaos

the birds were gone

they looked at each other
faces lit with inner joy

such a satisfying moment
every year

the saving
of the cherries
by the seasonal cat

weather forecasting

I saw a plume
in the sky —
a quill of sorts —

writing

    storm

the wind was high
the clouds came in
much lower

grey grew wide
lightning
illuminated each letter

and the rain
washed the word
away

~

I saw a plume
annotating one section
of sky

the line it penned
in a trail
of white . . .

    sun

the blue
held the word
in a sweet formation

frayed slowly
by the zephyr breeze

Summer 2016

tailed away

~

I saw the impression
of a fading feather

neat . . .

perhaps a hackle

crisp lines
disappearing
the remnant
of a declaration

     burn

the sun
beat down

the sky filled
with wriggled lines
of an illusion

that there may be
water

learning to read by inches

he is learning
to read
one inch
at a time

he knows the words
he sees
the sentences
he can take in
and tell you
by the page

but he has never learned
to read the words
meaning by meaning

image
from page
to mind
as though a real thing
had just happened. . .

could
just happen

if he reads it right
the next inch
of words
holds a picture

if he can only *see* it

so he reads
once
goes back to read the same lines
again
and then
returns

Summer 2016

he isn't satisfied
any more
with *knowing*
a story

he needs more

he needs
what every inch of words
might hold

honking to be one

when the eggs cracked —
after a month
more
of mother duck
sitting —
his was
the second

his brother
extracted
before him

when mother walked
with all the brood in a line
to the stream
he wasn't first

in the water
he was just a little
slower

when it came the time
to fly . . .

he watched the way
his brother rose into the air
before he followed

and it was a gift
the way his wings
could steer through the sky
the power he felt
and the way he knew
where he was
all the time

superb
at landing

after his brother

autumn came
the flocks began to leave
the V's spread across the sky
as the sun rose

and he rose too
on the right hand side
just behind
his brother

he wondered then —
early in the flight —
if it shouldn't be
the best flyer
at the point
of the V

he wondered
what it would be like
if that were him

> *honk*
> *honk*

ruffling the skin

she cuts the stalk

trims the beard away

friseur
to alliums

ruffles the skin
until the loose
flakes the air
like
rice paper

like tissue
torn away by breeze

until the purple
stripes the bulb . . .

taughtened
to a stroking touch
that brushed it
clean

Summer 2016

trade-ie wars/replacing a water heater

no
you're wrong about that

I am not it was . . .

yes
you are

~

two old men are arguing
they are both old *tradies*
one a plumber
the other an electrician

one is obstinate

the other
is bombastically
arrogant

they have fallen into reminiscence

~

no
the end pipe was covered over

you're wrong
it was buried
in the dirt

~

the subject
is a hot water heater
they had occasion to work on
together

the debate . . .

whether a pressure relief valve
had caused the heater
to balloon out at both ends
putting life and limb at risk

etc

they are *tradies* and therefore
their work was always
of earth shattering
significance

~

look
I can remember
exactly

the pipe had been covered over
by the owner
with some . . .

>   *no*
>   *it was actually nose down*
>   *in the dirt*
>
>   *that's why it couldn't . . .*

~

they have each grown voluble —
shouting
without actually yelling —
trying to express
the loudest opinion

as though it mattered

worthy of war

~

Summer 2016

three of us
are seated at the table
in silence

one by one
we each roll our eyes
as we catch each others gaze

one leans across to ask

> *when did this*
> *water heater*
> *happen*

another smirks

> *oh*
> *about forty years ago*
>
> *they haven't worked together*
> *since*

a fisher of storms

at the prow
he stands —
waiting —
above the waters
swirl and turmoil

the movement
is a maelstrom

the whirlpool
is a shoal

down
in the teeming
he sees one . . .

it is the one he wants
to know

and he dives
casts his heart into the water
before him
held sharp and pointed
like the spear
of his intention

deep
deep down his diving

and far
far away below

eye on the prize

one —
the only one —
in that entirety of teeming

a thrust —
sharp —
of his spear point

Summer 2016

what has he caught . . .

he cannot know
until he rises

he can look then
at his prize

back onboard
and sailing
again
across smooth oceans

ever on

ever on
to distant storms

storm free

the storm
was nearing

gusts of singing wind
sounded
then softed
and silenced
while —
higher up —
the sky was a-scud
with the movement
of billows
and frowns

he removed all his clothes —
except the red jockettes —
and wandered outside
in the middle
of a still moment

lay down on his back
in the centre
of a small patch
of lawn
and waited

there had been heat
this day
and the breeze —
at first —
was tepid and slow
barely enough
to ruffle

but a sharp lick
saw the goose-bumps rise

harbinger
of the cold front

Summer 2016

the chill held him
to a shiver
and he almost leapt
into air
as a first fat droplet
struck his chest
before a pattering
caused a kind of prone
skeleton dance response
where cold kissed warm

but finally
it was serious

rain falling steadily
wind crying a chill
fierce lament
and he —
thoroughly soaked now —
releasing his awareness
to rise up
into the weather

so constant
the deluge and the buffeting
he found it difficult
to breathe
as he was beaten
and beaten again
all over

he wanted to laugh —
so thoroughly
was he purged —
but a small thing
inside
restrained him
whispering

> *you're going to drown yourself*
> *you bloody*
> *bloody*
> *fool*

absent friends *(snap)*

he said he didn't want
his face
to be in a photo

he said
he always seemed to wear
a vacant look
when his picture was taken
unawares

he said he'd put his hand
over the lens
to stop me getting a picture
but I snuck one
anyhow

I snapped it
when he didn't know

I didn't stop
to adjust
the focus
just pointed and shot him
while I could

but when I looked
at the picture
he wasn't there

well . . .

his body was
his jeans
his shirt
his jumper

his hands were holding
something . . .

I don't know
what

Summer 2016

his hat
was just a baseball cap
with the beak
pulled right down low

but his face
wore such an empty look
that I could see the tv
behind him
in the place
where his nose should be

his hair was there
shaped around a space
for ears

the fringe hung lank
unsupported
by anything

I guess when he said
he didn't want
to have his photo taken
he really meant it

but I surely asyonished
when I saw
he wasn't there

he must have been
facing
some other way

gave me
his vacant stare

his blank look

here's
to absent friends

beneath the oak

that grand old tree
is a room
that is a place apart

I enter
beneath its branches
to be
somewhere else

it is quiet there

it is silent

the peace of place

a stillness
of the world outside its boughs

sulphur-crested christmas fools

the cockatoos
are swooping around

the plums
ripening yellow

and those sulphur-crested
snow-white fools
are practiced in the art
of bending balance
at the end of laden branches

nuisance . . .

oh yes
they are a nuisance

the pulpy mess
they leave below them
is no rose

but dotted
here and there
among the greenery

they are baubles
on the tree
with the one perched
at the highest point
in the designated role
of christmas tree angel

gaston, my canard, teaches fantasy

gaston
my tutor
is teaching imagination
and fantasy
using french words

> *il est facile d'apprendre*
> *le fantaisié*
>
> *le qwark*
> (quack quack)

yes *gaston*
my *professeur*
takes a gallic approach
to reverie

> *le*
> *qwa-wa-wark*
> (quack quack)
>
> *qwa-wa-wark*
> (quack quack)

he waggles his feathers
and quacks so fast
I haven't the
imagerie
to take in what he says
but
I see a mallard
strutting on the stage
so at least I'm learning
to *qwark*

> (quack quack)

Summer 2016

gaston
tries to teach me

    (quack quack quack)

to see all the things
un canard ought to see

    le qwark
    (quack quack)

    le qwark
    (quack quack)

gaston
at the lectern

    qwark (quack quack)

is trying his best

    qwark (quack quack)

but in my *fantaisié*
when I look
he's a canard

    le qwark

    le qwark

I on solid ground

there is a storm raging
across the heavens

I see the dark
destructive clouds
gather
swarm
and rumble

wind gusts
with the lash of driven rain

I feel the cut

I wear the blows
and still I stand

I
on the temple
of my home

I stand
inside my doors —
no room for storms

> *rage*
>
> *rage*

rage you
loudly
amongst the night
in your darkness
for I
am holding
to a flame
that shows me clear
who am I
and why am I

Summer 2016

I can stand
against your terrors
flashed white on black
across the heavens

for here —
on solid ground —
am I

an accusation boogie

the wind accuses

>*you-you-you you-you*
>*you did the crime*

>*you-you-you   you*
>(me?)
>*you did the crime*

oh no
it can't be me no
I was not there
at that time

>*you-you-you-you*

no-no-no
you've got it wrong

>*you-you-you-you*

no
can't you see you're wrong

>*it's you-you-you*

no-no your case
isn't even very strong

>*well who-who-who   who-who*

the wind demands to know

>*who-who-who*

(not me)

*who was it
do you know*

no-no
I cannot say

for she would not speak to me
ever again
and then she'd take
my heart
away

(so sorry
mister wind)

artist enough

if I were
to brush

to oil

what would I
to word

is it
come one come all
or is there room for . . .

no

no

I will not
with brush
and I will not
with oil

I am *already*
with pen

how much can I need
can I use
can I want
can I be

I speak
I say the word

write the thought

look into
my own mind

look
right into yours

Summer 2016

what need to paint my reply
when I can speak
the word

I am
I am
my words

ping pong, under certain conditions

there are special rules
for special players
and for special games

a wing tip

a flipper

both double up
as paddles
with which to strike the ball

each
is painted to highlight
the sweet spot

legs that waddle
a tail
to propel a player
into his preferred position

a regulation table
dull green
white lined and ruled up
according to
interstellar standard

suspended in the ether

    game on

the dolphin
spins his serve viciously
sliding on the diagonal

skimming
just above the net

Summer 2016

dart forward
the duck
a sharp slice
to forecourt left

crosscourt the dolphin . . .

a little high
perhaps

    smash

the duck
without mercy
pounds the celluloid ball

eludes the dolphin
who cannot make his ground
flipper
flashing through the nothing
at nothing

the ball is gone

the players —
as one —
watch the parabolic curve
and trajectory
of their ping pong ball
arcing through space
descending
into the maelstrom swirl
of darkness
below

a last ray of light reflects
orange
then the ball
is swallowed
down

and down

quack

said the duck

> *there goes*
> *another one*

> > *eck-eck-eck*
> > *eck-eck-eck*

came the reply

> > *you win*
> >
> > *let's start*
> > *a new game now*
> >
> > *you*
> > *have the privilege*
> > *of serving first*

green lady

she throws back her head
leaves hair
to stream out behind her

taken up
by the wind
in rustles and flutters

    sway

she dances without moving

    sway

breeze blow
zephyr
carry me *away*
with the dancer

the green lady

can't trust the rice

he is almost inarticulate
in his fury

almost desperate
in his need
to chastise her

>*how many times*
>*have I said*

>*when you're cooking*
>*you can't*
>*you mustn't*
>*do anything else*

>*how many times*

~

>*well*

she said

>*I thought*
>*both of you were right there*

>*surely you would know*
>*when the rice*
>*needed to be stirred*

>*to be taken off*
>*the flame*

>*why does it have to be*
>*my fault*

~

Summer 2016

he approaches me
afterwards

wheezing and breathless
from the exertion
and the expenditure
of so much emotion

>　*what am I going to do*
>　*with her*
>
>　*I can't trust her*
>　*with anything*
>　*anymore*

~

she approaches me
afterwards

eyes a little glazed
anxious
to have a private —
perhaps more sympathetic —
conversation

>　*I forget so much*
>　*these days*
>
>　*today I got distracted*
>　*by the washing*
>
>　*he seems to need*
>　*so much*
>　*to get angry with me*
>
>　*I do my best*

~

>　*all right*
>　*all right*

*let's just stop now
no more yelling*

*the rice is burnt
but no one has been harmed
you're both ok*

the saucepan will be cleaned

the smell will clear

*you'll eat a different meal
than you had planned*

*this afternoon
you rest*

both of you

*I'll come back
tomorrow*

and we'll start again

*hoo roo
till then*

two totters

she totters
when she walks

it's as though her heels
could be stilettos
even though she's actually barefoot

no matter the footwear
the totter-gait remains

perhaps due an uncertainty

> *of medication*
> *of weight*
> *of life preoccupied*
> *lived in her mind*

the first totter
is slow
pronounced and ponderous

a little bit

> *drunk at the end of a long day*
> *at the races*

careful

her mind is busy

> *a complaint*
> *about the absence of a cigarette*
> *(a request*
> *to which she knows the answer*
> *is already*
> *no)*

a threat
that failure to deliver on this important demand
means that she
will simply have to die
before dinner is served
on christmas day

it is a thoughtful
ungainliness

totter two
though
is a dance step
there is jaunt
and
there is precarious haste

happy christmas!

joy to all

potato chips with honey soy
an ice cream
and . . .

an extra cigarette

interpreting signals

waiting

the clouds are grey
massing above us

filling the horizon
away to the west

lightning —
untranslated semaphore —
is sending messages
of what the heavens have in store

if only
I could understand them
these signals flying all around me
in the telegraph line
that is the air

but I am blind

I cannot see them
I am deaf
I cannot hear
illiterate
I cannot read the portent
of what the stormfront has said

so
I wait here
with those few senses
that I own
open to the sky
waiting for the weather to show
with a kiss on my skin
from the wind
with a wet touch
fallen from a droplet
of rain

I am waiting

the clouds
away in the west
are grey

Summer 2016

twice packing the pigeons

he has always kept pigeons
pure white
in their innocent pomp

they are table birds
and he has harvested the young
as is the way

cleaned
the carcasses will be frozen
she will gladly enough pluck the birds
after slaughter
but will not eat them

it does not feel right to her

and he has no appetite
to for them today

hardly an appetite
at all
but
what else
is there to do

~

he is engaged
breathlessly
on the telephone

she is fiddling open
a sealable plastic bag
for the freezer

clumsy

she struggles a half of a bird
into a bag

another bird
another bag
but this time
it is a whole bird

a small bag

fiddle
push
study

push again

    look out

he wheezes in a whisper
free now
of the phone

she hears something
but
has mislaid the hearing aid
and simply stops what she is doing
gazing quizzically at him

he makes a move
to occupy her place
at the bench

she gives way
a little reluctantly

he is shaking
a tremor
that is all about the effort involved
in catching breath

~

he removes the pigeons
from their bags
where she has placed them

repacks steadily
despite vibrating —
almost oscillating —
hands

> *there*

they are ready now
for the freezer

he visibly relaxes
although the effort involved
in the intake of his air
remain intense

she has moved away
and is focused intensely
on new challenges

> *where*
> *are her glasses*
>
> *what has happened*
> *to the walking stick*

these things are slippery
in their elusiveness

shopping

every day
he goes shopping
in the afternoon

he can't go
in the morning

it takes a long time
to wake up
these days

the burden of a shower
is an exhaustion
that lasts
beyond the towel
beyond
a shave and the donning
of a singlet
the putting on
his outdoor shorts

he'll lean awhile
on the kitchen bench
deep
audible gasps
of stale
emphysemic air

while he reads
the gospel
according to his daily
tabloid

then navigates the cooking
to be ready
come lunchtime

> *twelve o'clock*
> *then serve*

is a tradition
that has become
a rule

a grandpa nap
and a quiet
lung-settling
in the easy chair
is the closest point to
no gasping
he can reach

but every day
he will go shopping
in the afternoon
at the self-service grocery
just off the main drag
where he can manage his laps
around the aisles
by resting on the arm of the trolley
when he needs
some air

at the lotto shop
he'll seek out
convenient parking

a *quickpick* ticket
is eighteen lines
of random numbers
that offer a fortune
he neither needs
nor wants
except

it's important

you have to know
that you're still
in it

it is something to speak of
each evening
over a beer
at the local pub

but
pharmacy for steroid pills
and inhalers
is a little bit more challenging

there's always
some prick there
in the *disabled parking* space

so he drives around the block —
there are four turns
to every square —
to bring him
back again
for another hopeful look

no space . . .

what to do . . .

go around again
dear sir
go around again

or
just go home

try again
tomorrow

Summer 2016

elements of the tapestry

needle says

> how stuck am I
>
> I believe
> I've lost the thread
> that holds me
> to my life

cotton
strings along

> never mind
>
> never mind old friend
>
> I am
> still with you
> here
>
> over and under
>
> through and through

linen waits

outlining half stitched ideas
in dreams
clean and white
but —
so obviously —
crumpled

there is a tapestry
waiting for a chance
to emerge

filling up with colours
shaded blue

shaded green

a depiction of water
halted mid-stitch
on account of the heat

an *out of season* idea
melted
like a snowflake

gone
without leaving so much
as a watermark

fading away

Summer 2016

time awareness

      what is time

he doesn't know

something *then*
is different *now*

if tit is he same
then . . .

he
is what has changed

an idea
that shapes
everything

everywhen

      does time change

      when
      and how is that achieved

      is it me
      that alters to accommodate
      a different
      now

I read somewhere
that someone —
some person full of wisdom —
has decreed

      one second

the year just past
had to be made *more*
by one second

is that —
can that —
be real

surely someone
is playing god

or timelord

how will *I* be changed
if they don't know
and
what *right* do they have
to tamper

I believed that time
was self-aware
enough
to do without
second thinking

Summer 2016

before her majesty

there is a child at babble
I can hear her
behind the fence

things are happening
because she says
they should

so they do

the few objects
before her
are neither plastic
nor toys

they are the towers
and pillars
of a new world

listen to her voice now

*murmuring
and low*

listen to her voice now

rising

I
listen to her voice now

*determined
satisfied*

what was wrong
is made right

what is right
is what she wants

the empress decrees it
and all of you —
in her dominion —
you better
bow
low

reek assessment

flat rock road
is on fire

I saw it
on the news

> *forty acres*
> *of grass*
> *forty acres*
> *of flame*
>
> *sky full of clouds*
> *sky full of smoke*

the one
is wet and grey
the other
dirty brown
and billowed

a helicopter landed

> *whocka-wock*

behind the fence

we all climbed
on moulded plastic
outside chairs . . .

craned our necks
to take look

the first fire
of january

first
of the year

Frank Prem

here it comes

the season
of assessing the quality
of grey
for the brown reek
of smoke

hot one

the hottest day

only the yellow
of a buttercup
is holding steady

everything else
is wilted
and looking about ready
to die

the sun is no friend
he has set his mind
to burning

I'd try to look him in the eye
but
I think
he would leave me
blind

the shade
beneath the oak tree
is a world
in a cocoon

the temperature in there
is set to

    ahhh

the lake
is not so far away . . .

a little later
I think I'll go in

talk to the sun
in bubbles
from underwater

a small breeze
ruffles leaves
up high

if it should decide
to visit
a little lower

maybe . . .

maybe
we'll survive
to the end
of the day

let the runners run

the cucurbits
are away

pumpkins have spread
outside their circle

the white squash
has raised
a yellow flower
but trails behind
zucchini
which sends fruit out ahead
and puts a flower on top

a little *carmen*
miranda

at last
the cucumber looks like
it might get serious

it considered
for awhile
whether it might prefer
simply to die

tomatoes have settled in
ready to sprawl
or to dance themselves
around a supportive pole

such *sexual* creatures

the new strawberries

each wears one off-set flower —
adornment fashion —
this time
perhaps
from tahiti

sweet potatoes
are planning paths

the bed is theirs
to claim

melons have survived
their uncertainties
and I think they are sure now . . .

possibly

so let the runners run
the sprawlers sprawl

let the climbers
reach
for the sky

this is summertime
so
let the flowers show

autumn will be here
soon enough
to kiss these running times
goodbye

Summer 2016

picking wild sunshine

picking plums
right off the branch
is not
what most people do

not anymore

but I've got a tree
growing wild

it is wide
and it is high

and it is bent down
beneath its load

I have sunshine
captured
in my bucket

it has come down from the sky
into the plums
and then . . .

to me

picking sunshine
right off the branch
is not a thing
most people do

but
I
have have it
brimming
in my bucket

transcribing from the original

four-two-wit
four-two-wit
four-two-wit

I am capturing
the lyrics

but . . .

I don't know

really
I don't know
whether I can decipher
them into words

wardle-ordle-ordle-ordle
yordel-odle-odle-orrr—orr
wardle-ordle-ordel
yordle-odel-odel-ey

perhaps *this*
is close

idle idle idle-idle
I am idling in sunshine
idle idle idle
I am idling away

I have just tried singing
the untranslated copy
aloud
outside

the magpie uttered a comment

> *nyark*

twice

> *nyark*
> *nyark*

then flew off

inconclusive
to my mind
for *that* particular bird
is only a youngster

I wonder how close I came
to the original
with my
enunciation

I thought
it was pretty good

axeman: a philosophy of the woodpile

sometimes —
like life —
a *round* of sawn wood
is too hard

>*will it be*
>*the axe*
>*or the splitter*
>
>*perhaps the wedge*
>*and a hammer*

sometimes
there is no way
through the knot

if you take the round
at the outer
you can slice
after slice
it apart

but what of the gnarl
that lies
a tangle of curling fiddleback
in your path

can you
smite your way
home
like a god
wielding his hammer

and what
when the wood
holds together despite you

Summer 2016

does that crack
there
lead right through
the centre

or is it just a trap
to tempt you away
from the tried and true journey
around the edges

do you smash it
to splinters
determined in your rage

or move on

throw the ugliness
of mauling
to the discard pile
with the rest

truth holds

truth holds

whether you can find it
or no

its in the hard rings
tight around the centre
of the heartwood

and it will bathe you
like a swimmer
in a bucket
of sweat

that's the lesson taught you
through the thin edge
and smooth handle
of your splitter

a-wooing for coffee

yellow bourbon e-
special

ethiopia yirgacheffe as well

green beans to brown
oily smoke
and the *cra-cra-crackling* sound

coffee over the stove-top

espresso
I desire

here is a batch of beans . . .

green-to-brown them

turn the heat much
higher

grind to start the day right
percolate the morning growl

give me give me give me
coffee
don't make a grown man . . .

a-a-a   a-wooooo

a-a-a   a-wooooo

don't make a grown man

a-wooooo woo-woo-woo

for my
coffee

scent of ambrosia

praise the smell
of peaches
rising
up from the bowl

not quite ripe
just yesterday
today
they fill the whole room

have you smelt
the peaches

hold a moment . . .

inhale them right now

let them fill
your senses
with the fragrance
that is all around you

>   *peaches*

>   *nectar*

>   *peaches*
>   *ambrosia your name*

today
they fill
the whole room

***thwock*-ing turbulence**

the *thwock*-ing
of a copter blade
luffed my ears
and echoed
right through the house

I searched —
window
to window —
trying to locate the source
of the reverberation

    there

    high

an afterburn image
of blades spinning . . .

somehow
following themselves

always half a *thwok*
behind

and a ripple through the air
like petrol
in a state
of vaporization

a turbulence that troubled
even the smooth air
in the sky

headed north
away from me

maybe the cops
maybe fire
maybe
some kind of super-special
vip

going to somewhere
important

yeh yeh yeh
but not me

I'm for the nursing home
mother in the back seat
for a special-special
first ever time
delivery

see you later
heli-chopper
I've got to go
to try to calm
some troubled air
of my own

but turbulence
is more likely
and flying
just half a *thwock*
behind

the day away

the day
begins to die
as the sun
sends its light
out low

honey
and balm
lie long
across the lawn

and the heat is all gone —
there is none now —
and has become warm
as
the blood
swimming in my veins

everything calm

the world
is quiet
as the stillness
in the deep dark
of graves

trees stir
in a shiver
but nothing disturbs

the day passes
away
as the sun sets

on peaceful streets

today
they found anne frank's
pendant

after all these years
they're still sifting
through the traces
of old war
and cremation

in nigeria
they found a couple
of stolen schoolgirls —
babies at the breast

strangely
they've grown into women
and their sisters
are still out
in the wild somewhere

and who they might be
is lost
in the clouds of

    still
    at war

another little boy
bloodied
dragged out of the rubble

mosul
or *aleppo*
I can't even tell
they all look the same

another city another child
both broken

here at home
we have no war
but the refugee children
are setting up in gangs
riding the night
ram-raiding the day

>   *hammers*
>   *machetes*
>   *guns*

they have grown up
these war children
to re-teach the lessons
of kid survivors everywhere
out on peaceful streets

>   http://www.foxnews.com/science/2017/01/15/israel-says-nazi-camp-excavations-unearth-link-to-anne-frank.html
>
>   https://en.wikipedia.org/wiki/Chibok_schoolgirls_kidnapping
>
>   https://en.wikipedia.org/wiki/Ram-raiding

floe

there is a floe
drifting the sky
bunched up
separated
encompassing pinpoints
of light
as it drives
to the last fade
of the sun
leading
as west as if
gravity
resides down there
just a small way
beneath that horizon
they sail
serene
in their ocean
under
their stars

wearing *down*

through the morning
he watched
the creation of a cloud
from traces
glimpsed on the horizon

slowly
sailing forward

growing
billow
upon billow
of feather-filled
soft curves

high on high
an accumulation
of roundness

voluptuating beauty
in low sun

a seduction
wearing
feather-down

sound returns

>*brrraaaaoooooowwwooottt*

>*broooowwaaaaoooottt*

sound travels
beneath the water

>*brrrooowwwooottt*

slow waves
long distances
high speeds

>*brrrreeeewwwooottt*
>*buurrrroooowwwoottt*

and the sound
of waves
bouncing off coral
washing on beaches

returns

>*brrrrwwwwwooooorrrrtttt*
>*brrrooowwrrrrttt*

last

what is
a *last breath*

he imagines a scene

> *ice-light*
>
> *blackness and blue-white*
>
> *a grizzled figure*
> *male*
> *with hands folded*
> *over his chest*

he can almost feel
the imposing dead-weight
of the folded hands
and arms
across his own chest

restricting the freedom
of his own diaphragm
and lungs
to take in
the necessary quota
of air

and as he watches
in increasing self-discomfort

> *a white mist*
> *rises*
> *from the pale mouth*
>
> *suspended*
>
> *for a moment*
>
> *then thins*
> *disperses slowly*

Summer 2016

is that
it . . .

maybe

but he wonders too
if it isn't also the gradual
stifling
and suffocation
of choices

narrowing with age
and the barely-suppressed awareness
of an unswayable
forward creep
towards infirmity

and the tease
of fleeting memories
whose laughter
each day
he hears
and feels
more pointedly

more distantly

what is it
really

the *last breath . . .*

he doesn't know
not really
but
can imagine

how (to hell)

the golden rule
when she was small

> *everybody will care*
> *for their own*

and the old and young
lived side by side

the young took roles —
much bigger —
as the elders
faded into their yester-days

they fed them
from the garden plot

the youngsters played
around their feet

another way
of making sure
they were
ok

the old ones
fed the geese
and hens

and rocked in corners
beside the fire
as evening fell

these were the ways
the young
showed respect and love
for the elders

~

Summer 2016

here she stands
clutching tight
to a walking frame

the sliding doors
glide open
every time she moves

but she will not
go forward

she does not believe —
cannot believe —
she has yet come so low
as this

they *say*
it is only for one week

they *say*
she can go back
to home

but she knows
that —
though they may mean
what they say —
there is no truth
inside the words

she knows
that she will not
go back

she knows *they* won't
allow it

they will wrap her up
in common sense

they will cloak her —
choke her —
with all their *reasonables*

so

how did life descend
to such a bleak
abyss

did she really fail
to love them
to care enough for *them*
to love *her*

to keep her at home
where old folk
still
can look after the hens

can pull a weed

can doze
when they are tired
in the afternoon

how did life –
that seemed so good –
go straight
to hell

voices know (wo-wo-wo)

the voices in the wind
are talking

> *oh wo-wo-wo*
> *oh-wo wo-wo*

every time
I think I know
what's really
going on

> *wo oh-wo-wo-wo*
> *wo-wo oh-wo-wo*

quiet
for a moment

nothing
for a spell

I think I understand it
but. . .

no

> *oh wo-wo-wo*

the wind knows better

> *wo-wo-wo*

I know
nothing

> *wo-wo-wo*

and nothing

oh-wo

is all I
am allowed
to know

in the cloud

the wings
of a lonely locust
flash yellow
in the sun

he traverses
green
he traverses brown
then
the search for a mate

in search of a mate

in search of . . .

he has to find his mate

yellow wings
the locust flies
lost
in the middle of his mates

lost amongst his mates

yellow wing
is lost

in the cloud

all mates

eucalyptus farewell

an old windmill
across the back fence
is twirling
like it is powered
by the current
from a river
of the wind

around and around
while the branches
high above
are waving
their eucalyptus *fare-thee-well*

>*bye and bye*

>*bye and bye*

>*we'll see you*
>*a little bit later*

there has been a promise spoken
that the rain might come
tonight
or maybe
early in the morning

when I look up at the sky
the clouds look full
but the air is holding
only the memories
of a burning sun

while the humidity
is enough
to broil me

but the trees
keep waving

so long

so long

so long and singing
a sweet shush
to the wind

bye shush-aby

*and goodbye-bye
shush-aby*

*we'll see you
in the morning*

*we'll see you
later*

bye shush-aby

*I
will see you
later*

shush-aby

returnee (the heroine of there and back)

my lizard has returned

I —
rather sadly —
watched her leave . . .

it must have been
weeks ago

I didn't know
where
or why
or if
she would reappear
pretty in her stripes
tongue
licking blue-ly
at the air

fixing me —
wary —
with a reptilian look

I do believe
she seems to be
a little bit
larger
than before

standing on the veranda
checking out
whether I
am moving

friend
or foe

I turn away
look back
she is gone

Summer 2016

lizard is there
no more

but her trek
is complete

I will meet her again
basking in the sun
stretched out on some bricks
giving me
the lazy eye

her journey
took her away

now it has lead
back home

mock orange

tangerine

sky

the day —
today —
was a stinker

every time I saw the sun
it burned me

every time
I looked into the orb
I went blind

now tangerine
the sky —
so benign —
is nothing but a stinker

there is no apology
no *why*
no promise
to put its ire
away

just a passive/sweet
good night
splayed in orange
across the face
of the clouds

a sweet mock
left behind
to remind me

left behind
only
to tease

Summer 2016

a towel to ride

cum-eer-cum-eer cum-eer-cum-eer
cum-eer

would you look at this

the frenzy in his summons
interrupted her reading

he was
standing at the glass door
staring out
at the washing line

a pair of magpies —
juveniles
still grey
much more than black
short beaks
and sharp claws —

hanging
a-twirl
upon two towels
draped
around the backyard hoist

ride
little magpies
you ride

let the breeze
spin you
around

ride
little magpies
ride
it will only be
for a short while

air china

*I ain't a-gonna break
at least
until I hit the floor*

*ain't a-gonna break
at least . . .*

it was a little like . . .

no
it was *exactly*
like flying

what matter
if it came from
a slip
a push
a fall

a *leap*

the rush of the air
was an
exhilaration

and the song
a spontaneous joy

short lived but
oh
such life
such fast
fast life

*I ain't a-gonna break
at least
until I hit . . .*

persepctive

is this
perspective . . .

I stand below the branches

big and strong
tree trunks
they climb
and dwindle

split
into a map-work
of arterials
and splinter tracks

of leaves
and distant destinations

.

.

.

I believe
there may be blue
up there

the pictured book

she laboured
long days
with the brush

 hard cover

rich brown

 dust jacket

colourful . . .

lurid

title
author
publisher

 spine

all details
all important

this book would be judged —
after all —
by its cover

 inside front

jacket blurb
and precis

 inside back

author bio
a picture —
her portrait —

index

and chapter headings
page numbers

roman numerals
in the preliminary pages

blank

chapter one

in some ways
easier now

each word water coloured
to read crisp and clear

so much text
so many characters

so much story

but
there is a pattern
a rhythm
to paint/write
and she is able to progress

each page
it's own painting
each word
a small art

and this book

beloved

news

I get my daily news
from the *national voice*
even though
the government has one foot
hard-pressed upon its throat

I still —
most of the time —
trust it

I take my daily news
from *the eon of our times*
even though
the paper is grown so thin
while the advertisements
remain so large
and very wide

I am still —
from all my reading life —
accustomed to it

I take my daily news
from *the goggle-face online*
even though
my eyebrows have risen high
and the things it says
just take my breath

I can't believe
yet so many
cite it
gospel true

i take my daily news
from the sulphur crested cockatoo

Summer 2016

even though
it screeches its opinions
so loud

so very garish

at least I know
its point of view
is just
bullshit

song rules today

there is a concert
in the garden

magpies
sing after a storm

they *wardle*
voice transformed
into song
completely

carolled thoughts
in softened sunshine

the *afterwards*
of rain

wind sings
its *passing-by* lines

a moan
and wail
as it joins in

but the magpies
sound
more loudly

no wind-song will rule
today

resident wind

the song of the wind
is weeping

on this day
no consolation
will suffice

tearing hair
a wail that whips the branches

my old oak
is shedding leaves
as though they were tears

for the wind
is howling through wires
like a banshee

for the wind
is moaning low
in grief

this wind-song is either
a whirl
and a whip and a cry
or
a lowing of loss
and of woe

wo-wo-wo

oo-oo-oo

wo-wo-wo

oo-oo-oo

this wind
is a resident
inside me

wo-wo-wo

oo-oo

it is singing
inside my head

benedicted by the day

cockatoos
a-flutter in the sky
like a string
of prayer flags
taken wing
beneath a sun
that alternates
the white
of whisp-ing clouds
with the sky
of deepest blue

a screech of supplication
and a moaning
from the wind
set a reverence to the day
and a warm bask
upon my face
like heaven with a glow
reached town to touch
we worshipful
with our faces raised
to receive the benediction
that only comes
to the few of us
so blessed

my love tonight

shiraz love

I'm hoping for some
shiraz love

a clean-skin so pure
it won a medal

> *beat a cabernet sav*
>
> *outpointed some old
> bland merlot*

and I've got it by the case
in my cupboard
with no label

I've got it —
ruby red —
when it I hold it
to the light

shiraz love

tonight
I'll crack a bottle
for some
shi-
raz
love

> *chin chin*

Summer 2016

the green and the brown

o my beans of green

o my beans of brown

these are
coffee days

am I the master
or the slave . . .

I turn you on the flame
I
make you change

but
should I miss
a roasting
day
I
am a devastation

o my browning greens

o aromatic wonders

I turn you
round and round
that you should not burn

your oil lingers
fragrant
on my fingertips

the essence of you
is everywhere
and I
am the one consumed

line dancers

there you go
my sweetling dancers
there you go

trip along
to the song played
whistling
by the wind

around and around
fly your skirt
a-jig for an hour
and whirl yourself
around me

under the applause
of the sweep-by clouds
around and around

dance
around and around

under the applause
come
dance yourself
around me

not today

I did not read today
not a single word

when I tried I found
my mind veered off
to think of
other things

like

> the grass
> needs mowing
>
> and the wood
> needs stacking
>
> and the vegetables
> need water
>
> and the dogs next door
> are barking
> really loudly

I did not write today
not a syllable

when I tried to pen a line

> a poem a song a story

my mind
veered off
to think of
other things

like

> the horror
> of my government

*and the troubles
of my ageing folk*

*and the work at home
that I need to do*

*and the way my head
has started
throbbing*

so I'm sorry

very sorry

but I didn't
read

or write

today

Summer 2016

sweet blow-in

you blow in
ruffle my hair as you go

kiss me cool
so that I shiver

I close my eyes
to hear you
sing your song

you are the wind

I ride your voice
with every rising

sweet

>*touch me gentle*
>*all over*

sweet

>*touch me again*
>*to my heart*

sweet

>*your honey breath*
>*upon me*

sweet sweet sweet

>*luff me more*
>*breeze of mine*

you blow in

you ruffle my hair

power talk

the hum sounds
low
as it traverses
the wires

speaking in whispers
just for itself

indifferent to me
uncaring
of the howl
when the wind calls
it mutters alone
of traveling
free

freedom
in the low hums
and in the high crackles

it sings to itself
away
down the long wires

power lines

I ride the lines
I hum
and murmur

I see the moon
open it's eye
in the middle of the day

to watch me

I am filled
with the crackle —
the subdued roar —
of power

and I ride the lines
today
any way
that I want

>   *fuel me up*
>   *coal me*
>   *until I am red-glowing*
>
>   *make me hot*
>   *heat me till I'm ready*
>   *to blow*
>   *my*
>   *mind*
>
>   *turn me loose*
>   *I will ride these lines*
>   *to forever*
>
>   *turn me loose now*
>   *I am humming*
>   *ready to go*

I ride the lines
half moon watching
above

yes
watch me

by day
by night
I am power
and these
are my roads

bear in

I am known
as *bear*

I roam the woods
and the forests
of your mind

seeking bright-eyed
berries
shucking husks
from ripened kernels
catching salmon-ated dreams
as they leap
to try evasion
of my grasp

even when I'm sleeping —
call it *winter*
if you will —
I keep an eye
half-open
to stay in touch
with what you do

excuse me
if I snore —
if I disturb
your subtler thoughts —
but
I am known
as *bear*
I roam your forests

and if I occasionally
interfere . . .

well
I have never
intended harm

I scrape my claws
I scratch my back
against the trees
and shrubs
left along your path

can you hear me . . .

sometimes
can you feel me . . .

I am rumbling
stumbling
rolling
roaring
across the grass bent over
by your footsteps

I am your bear

I roam your mind

sniffing what you
are thinking
where you are going
what you have done

your woods and forests
your *big ideas*
everything you know
what you have left
behind

I stand alongside you
on your pinnacles
to survey the realm
we know

you in your way
I in *bear*-way

we watch over
the forest and the woods
that are our home

Summer 2016

size and stature

    I am small

my questions
encompass the sea

I am a grain of sand
who wonders
about the beach

the ocean

the ebb and rise
of her water

    I am small

my eyes
aim high

I cannot see
what a star looks like
but I can see
the bright spots in the night sky

the twinkling
above me

    I am small

my footsteps
are determined

I cannot walk
around the world
but I can make
this soil
something . . .

something
my own

my
familiar

    I am small

nothing
has the power
to daunt me

inspired to leave

the leaf —
attached as it was
to a spindling branch —
dandled itself
in the breeze
above the river

it had held on
for so long —
waiting
until it had grown —
watching all the time
as elders
first clung
and then released
themselves

and now as the breeze
came tempting again
singing its old shanty song
inviting
seducing
kissing
and whispering
urging to

>   *come on*
>   *let's go*

the leaf
not needing much
inducement
was ready to fly
then
to sail

and it twirled
on release
in the air

round and round

set its sights
on the river

sets its sights
for the middle
of that flow

> *so long old tree*
> *for everything*
> *I thank you*
>
> *so long green leaves*
> *such good friends*
>
> *I am on my way*
> *to the ocean*
> *so very far*
>
> *I have waited all my life*
> *to set sail*
>
> *and now*
> *I am flotsam to the sea*
>
> *farewell*
> *I leave you*
> *for the sea*

the leaf sailed high on the water
to the bend
and its friends
on their spindling branches
waved goodbye

and more than one
that day
made its mind up . . .

Summer 2016

when the time was right
to *let go*

and to try
for the river
then the sea

while the zephyr
sang its song

    come with me

at the social security office

there is a *greeter*
at the door

she must be full
of knowledge
to be able to direct all enquiries
to the right places
but —
when I stepped too close —
she looked instantly scared

backed away from me
as though I was a threat
in the process
of materialization

in the voice that they use —
the one that conveys
to you that the presence
of pimples
on the face
is an unbearable discomfort —
she seeks my details

I've forgotten to bring
my numbers
so
it has to be
the hard way

then

    sit over there

the headmistress

the wayward pupil

Summer 2016

one vast open-plan
office floor
filled with computer desks
each with two screens

chairs
times thirty
facing away from the working office

I am not to look until called

every chair
is a sickly green
is part of an arc
pointed across empty space
towards the window

and the street

there can be
no spying on the workers
no hint of agitation

irritation —
even irony —
might be subversive
and extract a punishment

> *how would you like*
> *a six week hiccup*
> *to kiss your dole cheque arriving?*

and finally . . .

my name
is called

and a complexity
of routine
and unspeakable boredom
is initiated

if I didn't know better
I would swear
this clerk was moving
mountains
for me

but in truth
the system is just
s
l
o
w
and she doesn't care much
but
there is a time allocated
for enquiries of my kind

it must be filled
without eye contact

it must be filled
with the authority
of government
and the law

did I mention
that the chairs
are the colour
of colic . . .

and the authority here
is moved by knowledge
of injustice justified
as routine

with an overlay
of the fear
of self-awareness

Summer 2016

don't mind the toll

there is a tolling
just on the outside of my mind

not the clangour of a grand bell
chimed from atop some steeple
with a name like

ethelred

no no . . .

this is more like
a rhythmic drip
of water
falling from the gutter
of a rooftop
through a downpipe
to *plink*
when it strikes the bottom
at the drain

no no
it's not like that . . .

it is the *boing*-ing
of a spring
slowly uncoiling
keeping cadence
to the unravelling of the bed
beneath me

no no . . .

it's just a random toll
sounded
altogether vaguely
just
on the outside
of my mind

in the room

there was nothing
in the world
but the room

silence inside
light outside

the sun —
greening
through leaves —
shielding the room
from life

a corner of blue
was the day
and on the river
of road —
flowing
just out of sight —
a wave-wash of cars
shoo-shoom
and swimming by

of trucks
gear-changing their thunder
into the atmosphere

in the room
there was nothing
at all
but the whole of the world

and the restlessness
of the universe
of every thing
remained outside

Summer 2016

making home

I will away
from here

into the easy breeze

unravel
a silk trail
behind

I'll fly
to find
a new anchor

—
 —
  —
   —
    —
     —
      —
     —
    —
   —
  —

oh
my shining line
my
gossamer

I see
where I have been

but here
I will weave
a home
for me

and I will tight
each cord enough
to sway
but never break
no
no
not even
though tempest rage

not under a baking sun
beating down
and down on me

I will —
from my inward dream —
sculpt

such a home

never again
will I leave

dragonfly summer

it's a dragonfly summer
four-wings
manoeuvring
above my lawn

zig-zag
in straight lines . . .

so
geometry in flight
is born

in a dragonfly summer
there is no room
left to fly

a zig
when there's a zag
and it's *bye bye*
dragonfly

dragonflies in summer . . .

flotillas

like a tattoo

the sun can look
right through them
gossamer
on the wing
for you

prepare your home

*check your doors
the winter is coming*

I've been where
the wind
weeps
and it moans

the song it wails
is a cold chill
and growing

one of these days
it's going to blow
through your home

*have you closed
the gaps*

*are your windows
shuttered*

listen to the wind
it is crying
be warned

I sing the song
together
with the wind
of winter

*oh
wo-wo-wo*

I sing along

Summer 2016

will you sing with me
from your warm

just watching
as the wind keens high
it's moan

    oh
wo-wo-wo

wo-wo-wo

sea, the desert

oh sea
separated
so far
from your water

always your waves
shimmer
dance
with promises
drawn from the deep

oh sea
I will drown
in your bed of dust clouds
and sand

I flounder
bereft of water
beached
and burnt
by your sear

of your heat

Summer 2016

like rain

from above
there is little to note

his progress is
steady
as though slowly moving
through snow

from below . . .

silver white
in an expanse
flecked with continent shapes
that stretch
seemingly forever

occasional blue patches
glimpsed momentarily
then swallowed up
again

it is when on the level plane
looking across
that he is revealed

his legs working
feverishly

frantic

a blur of motion
working

    updownupdownupdown

ceaselessly

hardly pausing in their
apogee-perigee
relationship
with the cloud

his momentum forward
is a stutter-step
like a wound mechanical

a clockwork toy
focused
on a breathless traverse
that will not tolerate

> *a stall*
> *a hiccup*
> *a hesitation*

driven

> *updownupdownupdown*

for should he stop –
suffer a failure
of impetus –
he knows

knows surely

he will fall

Summer 2016

red (betelgeuse)

betelgeuse is red
my shadow is grey

rigel is blue
night is dark

sirius
is a rainbow
scintillating in the sky

the neighbourhood
is quiet
even trucks are at bay

and the moon has abandoned
her usual places

perhaps
she'll be along soon

meanwhile
the yellow sun
is sleeping

and I
am staring up
at different hues

once upon a time
each star
was coloured white
and twinkles

a long wave

my poem today
is an empty space

where voice should be

.
.
.

there is silence

long waves
play the old hits
on a radio
push the weather
around the planet

but there is no wave
where my verse
should reside

just static charges
(by the proton)
for nothing

there is emptiness
where my poem should be

hello hello

is life alive
out there

hello hello

I hear the echoes
resounding
from better days

Summer 2016

recitals read
one
after another

> *hello hello*

> *hello hello*

where is my poem
today
I can only hear
the sounds of the space
that it used to fill

blown away
by a long wave

what did you do today

you
what did you do today

> *well I*
> *got abused*
> *by my mother*

and you
what did *you* do
today

> *I hospitalised*
> *my father*

she did it
for her own true sake
just to keep
some sense
of control

and I did it
for his very own good
he doesn't like it
but . . .

that's the way

it's just the way

you
what *did* you do today

> *I slammed the door shut*
> *of the old house*

and you
what did you *do*
today

Summer 2016

I put the key
in my pocket

where it will stay

and if the door doesn't
open up
again . . .

that's for the best

the key . . .

well I think it right
to keep it safe
in my control

> *hey*
> *what did you do today*
> *was it anything*
> *like me*

did you wander
to the nursing home
or the hospital

did you pull the shutters
closed
on old old lives
like I did

I bet you didn't

I hope you didn't

I wish
you never have to

like
today

Autumn 2017

march is here

here lies the month
of march

what will it hold for me

> *start autumn days*
>
> *end daylight time*
>
> *pretend-summer running on*
>
> *maybe tomatoes*
> *red at long last*

what will march hold
for me

the trees are just beginning
to turn from their green
into brown

the sun still squeezes heat
from its rays

and I sit in air con
though autumn has come
it still feels like february
to me

it still feels february
to
me

the gentle art

a gentle science fiction
has taken me from
small town
to the sky

it doesn't take much
to get me there
just a jet pack
and a helmet

perhaps no more than
a bubble
filled with oxygen —
and me —
that rises

rises
up

maybe
I just thought
the thought
of floating
above the blue orb

or
I only saw it
as a speck —
such as grit
removed from the eye
of *sol*

and spun away —

I believe that I imagined
me —
in a sleek and silver tin can
in some other galaxy —
suddenly
in the fight of my life

well
how about that
just a second out
of warp speed
and into a dogfight

    pow pow pow

in the middle of the darkest space
turning round . . .

running for home

so much for
gentle

science fiction
is the *seat of my pants*
because
the shields are down

    (oh no)

communications *off*
and no-one cares
about me

except
to shoot me
without hesitation
back to earth

maybe
to eat me

oh
the hell with this
science fiction

now
I'm going to turn my mind
to a yacht
in brilliant white
sailing on blue
smooth
as a dream

you and I

a peaceful harbor

and at night
the shooting stars
comprised
of the returning debris
of some
gentle science
fiction

a coffee break

I have come
for a minute
and stayed . . .

oh
half an hour

maybe more

perhaps . . .

perhaps a lifetime
in such a short while

I breathe it in
inhale the taste
and the aroma

then —
when I see myself —
I have changed

I am not so young
anymore
as I *should* be

I look around me
and behind the shock
I see . . .

nothing
has really changed
it is just me
in a mood
of reflection

although the clock —
ever relentless —
has moved on

and now
the time has come

and I must
go

    au revoir

I'll see you later

the next time
our paths —
like this —
cross each other . . .

perhaps
in another kitchen
when it will be
my turn

    to perc the kettle

    to spill the beans

    to warm the milk

my turn
again
to turn around
and wonder

    where
    did it go

    where
    have I been

goodnight colours

the colours of the sky
are grey
and red and blue
and rosy hued

old-man's-beard-ed cloud
looks just like
it is waiting
for the hand of god
to reach out
and down
to touch me

one by one
the lights
are fading into night

one by one
the colours
glow
intensely
before they go

    good night

    good night

to the shades
of an evening palette

    goodnight

the dark must come
but it cannot replace them

he dreams while the corvids dance

the alpaca guard
is lying down

alone

aloof
on his hilltop

he spits a stream
of cudded juice . . .

if llama can
alpaca *will*

down the slope
the blue-eyed jets
are eye to eye
and beaks touch

they are raven-walking
back and forth
in a sway
of black satin
sheen

a *carnevale* of colour
noir

on barren slopes
sheep huddle in a mob
beneath the shade
of a single tree
under the blazing sun
and gaze
in wonder

for the corvid tango
is a trance

an intensity
unblinking

stylized struts reflect sunlight
in the deep and lustrous
shades of shining night

an emu drones its jaw harp
while another booms
in rhythm

the third bird
swallows its amazement
at the latin steps

raising dust above
the undulating horde
of birds
each holding tickets
for the dance floor

above
the alpaca guard
on his small
tonsured tor
is lying down

with eyes closed
he chews his cud
and ignores the *click*
of claws
and the rising cloud
of earthen powders
that surrounds him
staining his *pristinely white*
to *vaguely ochre*

his pretty eyes
are tightly closed

he chews and dreams
the wild alpaca dreams
of the andes

alpaca dreams of heroes
standing tall
with llamas

in pursuit

he is chasing
a moment of brilliance

chasing
a gleam
a shine
that brightened a moment
on the horizon

so far away . . .

so near
he could almost reach out
to touch

~

a moment of
thought
bright and clear

he
is chasing
the story of how
pen can create *poem*

chasing inspiration

> *a telling*
> *an idea*
> *the seed*
> *of a tale*

~

he is chasing

> *I am chasing*

Autumn 2017

an intuitive moment

    an intuitive moment

chasing

    chasing

the air

    the air

the taste

    the taste

that burned

    that burned

right before him

    right before me

so near

    so near

so far away

    so far

he could almost hold it

    I almost held it

in the palm

    in the palm

of his hand

    of my hand

slippage

it changes
in a minute

slips across the bifurcation
from

> *what you know*
> *is true*

to

> *what happened*
>
> *when*

sea bed

sun
has marbled the water
into mosaics

patterns on the sand

fringe fronds
from decaying seaweed
wriggle
for a moment
as a wave heaves

while the fry-fish
spread before us
scattered by vibrations
when I splashed my foot

churned the sand

the waves
keep come-and-going

>   *sh-sh-sh*
>   *hush and hush*

wash golden clean
this sea bed

towards a naming

after all
the mother stays
afloat
in seas
sailing the mind

she is in the place
he once belonged

she
is the siren
in his heart

~

there is nothing here
but braying night
black vision
black noise
black heart
blackened hope
for what may yet come

he shines
the glow from a pointed arm . . .

his suit light
touches ground
to show the way another step
will lead him

how long
his arm will shine
he cannot know

cannot bear to ask

beneath his feet
the ground
tilts
upward

his suit shows
the signs of strain
but
another step —
dragged
through the unseen dust —
drives him
towards elevation

he can't see far
but
this is *mountain type*
his clambering
seeks the high ground
and when the peak . . .

then
he will rest —
the longest rest —
as systems fade

there may come a day
of better light
when his colour
contrasts
with the landscape

they will find
his suit
and then
they will find him

a lone guru
on the mountain top

perhaps . . .

he laughs
a choking laugh

> *. . . they will grid the point*
> *and give the [place*
> *his name*

the first to come
the first
to go

he lets the dust fall
from a tilted glove

the nascent days of vicugna air

he paused

    mid-meal . . .

    mid bite . . .

    mid
    chew

in the field
a stirring
among the birds

wings flapping
an ungainly interval
of thrash and flap
and run

    a duck?

    a goose?

    ibis?

no

    this time
    a heron

all beak and neck
and commotion

the large birds
appear to struggle
with the mastery of their craft

eventually
achieving lift-off
and something
rather more like flight
than reverse disintegration

the heron departed the field

    he bit

    he chewed

    swallowed

    regurgitated

    chewed again

if it is
so hard
for a heron
to rise
then *he* –
freshly shorn
and de-fleeced –
could not hope
to rise

he bit
again
into the lush grass
of his paddock
and contemplated

this
would require a great deal
of thought

goat dance #1

mostly
just grazing . . .

every so often
the bearded old billy
would look up
and around
then leap —
all fours
into the air —

land
with a clatter
on the hard ground

look around again

  blaaat

then he would trot
a few steps

  clash

into the old paddock tree
a fierce strike
with his horns

leap
clatter

  blaaat

trot
trot

  clash

Autumn 2017

leap
clatter

    blaaat

his tail bobbed

    up

    down

    in circles

it is never too soon
to start

to practice

leap
clatter

    blaaat

trot
trot

    clash

wind-jig day

the wild wind
is playing
the clothes
on the line

it spins them
as it whistles
a tune

in *cavort time*
the pegs
wooden and plastic
are clicking
like rogue castanets

trees have been swirled
leaves
have been twirled

it's a heady dance
of wind-sway
and tousling
in breathless delight

around and around
goes the line

> *the shirt plumped out*
> *like a spinnaker*
>
> *the pants are horizon*
> *to the plane*
> *of the ground*
> *as they flutter*
> *stretched taut*
> *and away*
>
> *away . . .*

until the lull

all
set down

stop the adrena-line

wave
gently now
at each other
for a moment of pause
in-between

then
a whistle
to sign
a new reel

around
and around and around
they go

around and around
on the wind

she shrills her tune
and there is none
can resist

one more time
go around

getting lucky

I was talking
to the lottery seller
about the old men
and women

how their dreams
of being *lucky*
continue on

he said

>they come in twice a week

>they come in
>three times

>an octogenarian quick pick
>with a string of games
>in numbered rows

>some for tonight
>some more
>for tomorrow
>and the regular syndicate entry
>renewed to play
>on saturday night

>jack comes in
>barely keeping up
>behind his walker

>ellen parks her scooter
>right outside
>the agency door

>what do they think
>they'll do
>if they get a jackpot

*it's not as though
they need material things
or to plan
for growing old*

*and it'd all end up –
I'm sure –
with their families
if they won*

*I think this buying tickets
and chatting –
here in the shop –
is all the social life that's left
for folk who feel
their usefulness
is gone
but
might return
the day that they get lucky*

*one big win
and everyone
will know them
again*

the eye

I do not sing
to spite the rain

I don't whistle
at the wind

the storm
needs no encouragement
from me

I do not make my moves
too sudden
and I don't make a sound
at all

I move so slowly
you cannot tell

I place my hands
to shift the air

and when the storm
spins around my head

I am unruffled
dry
untouched
by the tempest game

> *spin around*
> *you deep*
> *black cloud*
>
> *spin around*
> *the eye*
> *I am*
>
> *make a curtain*
> *from your rain*

Autumn 2017

let the wind blow
in my name
in the heart of you
I stand

dream hunt

the hunter stalks the plain

    I am trying to sleep

some days the chase yields only empty fruit

    I turn over in my bed

where has the good game gone

    I listen to the silence

the hunter eyes a barren waste

    I plump my pillow

he sees a familiar shape

    I try to lie still with eyes closed

there – his prey is waiting

    I imagine the calmness of nothing

he creeps
he leaps
he captures

    and drift a little way away

the hunter begins to dance

marliess-opolis

in the small universe
of *marliess-opolis*
we all wear our hair
in platinum blonde

we wear pale-face
for foundation

red lipstick

bright
red lipstick

we are a totter town

we wear *tight*
over our bulges

we sing soprano
in a tremolo
and we recall
almost
all the words . . .

almost
sometimes

trail markers let us know
where we have been

the rouged end
of a menthol fag

the crimson smear
around the lip
of a glass
we used

we talk a lot
in the village
of marliess-opolis

we speak over the top
of other voices
that we don't want to hear

they have no say
about what
is what
around here

when we lie down
upon our beds
in marliess-opolis

the lids on our eyes
tremble
in the light

we like to be
tucked in
before someone
turns out our light

and then
we go to sleep
just like a baby

and then we snore
just like a diesel train

and sometimes we wake up
lost
alone
in marliess-opolis

> *tell me*
> *who*
> *has stolen*
> *our cigarettes?*

finding the colour

tomato man
goes chasing the red

in
and under
green foliage

the tomato repels
but
he likes that aroma
of green
and he burrows
among unripe hands
of truss berries

to find *there*

and . . .

there

one *nearly* ripe
and one red one

seize
and twist

into the baggie

there will be red
for dinner tonight

there will be salad
with solanum flavours
and juices
to run
down the side of his mouth

the tomato pursuit
has found harvest
and the smell of the leaves
and the stems

the awareness that says

>   *here*
>   *be tomatoes*

is smeared and spread
across his hands
and his arms

the tomato man
has found red

the slap

it gathered itself
as wisps
formed in the sky

it grew

>	*tiny*

>	*small*

>	*larger*

wisps became whites
turned into greys

it cannoned around
inside the cloud
as tension rose

and when the light
shot forth

when the roar
had echoed round

when the world around
had shattered . . .

it fell

>	*into the wind*

>	*arced across the sky*

>	*pushed*

it blew into others
broke down
and then reformed

it fell
with the glee of a flier

until a man
on the ground
looked up
and for just one moment
saw

it fell
until collision
at last
struck like the slap
from an angry storm

weather war

a thundering army
is descending from the north

    [CLA-ASH}

    [BA-BA-A-ANG]

a thundering army
drumming as it rides
my way

    [BA-BOOM]

    [BA-BOOM]

they light the sky
the clash their shields
a thunder of an army
with lightning bolts
to wield

    [TA-RA]

    [TA-RA TA-RA]

the wind
runs before them

    [WOO-OO-OO]

the wind runs
before them

    [WOO-OO-OO]

and then the rain

    [TA-TI-TI-TI-TA-TA TA-TA]
    [TA-TI-TI-TI-TA-TA TA-TA]

it is *battle on*

    [TA-TA TA-TA]

battle on

on the green

in a daydream

gazing outwards
through the window
away
a girl danced
across his meadow

in sunshine

light
billowed her skirt
while she turned
and turned

a pirouette
on flowers
and on the green

as she danced
she stepped closer
he could see her
care-less
care-free

she smiled

a few rounds more
until she reached him
and laughed

took his hand
in her hand
as invitation

so he stepped
through the glass
into his neverland

twirling
around each other
they danced

over the flowers
upon the green

slaking the forest

there is a forest rising
from the cutlery drainer
on the sink

>   *green flips and ladles*

>   *white spatulas*

>   *the blunt ends*
>   *of sharp knives*

cutlery
are dangerous trees
in their random dulls
and sharps

their serrations

I do not hunt there
in that topsy-turvy verdancy
of shallow innocence

no

I find the smooth
of crockery
a better idea
for the slaking
of my hunger

orchestrated autumn

autumn snow
is coloured brown
and gold

falling
from the oak tree

the back yard
is leaf-blizzard
before the storm

whipper-wind
flays the branches

cumulo-grumpus
masses
the skies

a lightning fork —
from top
to down —
a staff
to conduct the show

unravelling the code

the genie's lamp

she muttered to herself knowingly
as though she had found
what she expected

what is it

she glanced at me

that you wish for

turning back to her work

a bowl

it is filled with fruit

more bounty?

perhaps
perhaps

she grasped my hand
pointed
at a pattern in the markings
down
at the bottom of the square

markings that only she
could identify

there

she said

a horse

higher up the page

> *that*

> *is the rider*

> *is it a fall?*
> *a separation?*

> *what of the gun?*

she threw my hand down
discarded
while she mumbled
half under her breath

then turned
looked up at me directly

pronounced

> *it is you*

> *I see your face*

> *the die is cast*

> *touch your finger*
> *there*
> *on the shadow*

> *the code*
> *will take you*
> *where you need*
> *to be*

she held a thin
deeply lined palm
face up
towards me

waiting for it to be blessed
in silver

one form of 'good morning'

the traffic flows
down mellish street
like water
rushing
towards a drain

trucks roll by
with gravel
in their voices

the pre-dawn dark
wraps a cocoon
of threads and sounds
around me
asleep
inside the lullaby
of diesel
sung
in deep bass notes
that touch comfort
through my sheets
into my chest
in small echoes
and the vibrations
of stir
and waking

the brakes are a hiss and clang
that speaks

>*good morning*
>
>*wake*

a shudder
and finally
I am aware
of magpies

in the trees
that line the street
and the lessening of dark
that is the sun
rising

of the second breeze

I saved the life
of an hour today

gave it a second chance
at meaning

to become something
more than just
so much time elapsed

and in the minutes since
I have seen the sun —
still rising —
shadows on the green
and glistens of dew on grass

I have heard the carolling
of magpies
the abrasions
of a cockatoo

a vibration of reflected life
that is a wasp —
yellow and black
turned into grey-shadow —
through the window
and onto my floor

fifteen minutes
are *re-lived* by now

a quarter of the time
I saved

there is value
in reliving
I know because
I took the time
to ask the question
of the second breeze

one step new place

if I am *here*
then
you
are *there*

the only place I know
that you
could ever be

    I step sideways

    I step back

you aren't there
not anymore

and the person
in your proximity —
who looks
something like you —
is a different being
who has never
shared a moment
like you and I
shared that moment
when I was
here

before I took that one step
sideways

one step back

renewable

the sun
renewed the sky today
brightened up the blue

    I feel warm inside

the wind moved
through the trees again

they shivered
before my eyes

    I feel warm inside

the waves washed clean the sand
all along the beach

left it bathed in sparkles

    I feel warm inside

the earth renewed itself
again
while I stood still
watching the day unfold
and I
feel warm
inside

go gather berries

go
gather yellow berries
from the wild tomato bush
that has sprawled
all along the fence-line there

bring nibble bites
of juice to me
small bites of *jus*
to trickle down my throat
dribble from my mouth

tiny golden cherries
little *lycopersicums*

> *as tart*
> *as sour candy is*

> *sweet*
> *as thickened sauce*

go
gather me those berries
those
yellow draperies
a-sprawl along the garden fence

wild
golden baubles

tomatoes
of mine

into sleep

a lamp
by the bed

way beyond midnight

silence filled
with the sounds
rattling inside
a *would-be*
not-quite
sleeper

the stillness
is a transportation
to another plane

the sense
of *middle night*
a touch
surreal

shadows reach across
the ceiling
in search of corners
seeking out a place
of full retreat

and the darkness
when it comes
will be a blessing

a boon

for weariness
at an hour like this
comes to the fore

so
just a last line now . . .

or two

to half complete
a semi-thought

before the journey
into sleep
resumes

a line of brothers

oh poem of light
I see you dancing

radiant
catch colours as they fall

once around a ray
you twirl the rainbow

and it is only me
that knows you
with my eye

poem of darkness
I feel you
embrace me

a shroud
to cloak me
reflectionless

a pool of jet
I swim —
a small way —
above your depths

only glancing once —
my head plunged low —
to glimpse your soul

my brothers
I am the pen
the quill
to catch your heart
upon my paper

in the scratching
of my pen
we each become alive

the lightest light

the dark

arm-in-arm

trope-on-trope

we
brothers
of the line

concerto

raindrops fall
like prancing footsteps

a scattered pattern
tapped across tin

above my head —
the thunder drumming —
a fall of dance drops

a staccato tune

players pass
in wave on wave
new notes pounding

a tattoo played

applause falls down
out of bowing tree tops

fading soft
with the passing
of the rain

speaking of this and that (after the fall)

so I'm standing there
with my mother on the ground –
fallen from height
faceplant
onto the concrete –

waiting for an ambulance

my father wheels up
wheezing like vader –
emphysema
and a totally enclosed
self-centre –
says

>   *how much rain*
>   *did you get*
>   *last night*

I'm looking at my mother
lying full stretch –
she's stopped bleeding now
but you can see where her head
kissed the brickwork –

>   *oh*
>   *about thirty mils*

he says

>   *yeah?*
>   *well someone I know*
>   *said 31*
>   *so*
>   *that sounds right*

my mother says

Autumn 2017

oh
oh
where is the ambulance
won't somebody
help me now

oh
oh
oh

I hold her hand —
pat her head
try to put a cushion
underneath
to support her —

    and what about

he says

    what about
    this health insurance

    should I drop it now?

    we won't need it
    anymore

    it's so expensive
    I don't think
    we can afford it anymore

my mother
looks like she wants to say
something like

    oh
    woe
    oh

    won't somebody help me now

*oh
woe*

I am in pain

and so
I'm standing there —

after the fall

before
the ambulance —

and I don't know
what to say but

*oh
woe
oh*

*can somebody
help me now*

seeing through

I can see
through the trees
when the sun lines up
right behind their leaves

the transparent plum
of morning
shines golden green
to greet me

waving

    hello hello

I see
through the luminous
into the trees
of morning

yellow blue

I know the sun
is yellow
but it is striking me with blue
turned transparent
by the fall
from sky to me

from heaven
to my face and arms

so warm

so very
blue

I know the sky
is blue
but
it's striking me
with sunshine
I feel yellow rays transporting me
to *eyes closed*
and *face up*

    yellow warm blue

the sun

    strike me coloured

willing the oak

I have willed the oak tree
to show its leaves again

grey-green
against the sky
so blue
in radiance . . .

I half-close my eyes
unwillingly

I cannot watch the day

so still
except for morning birds
drifting in air
seeking places for song

parrots call
belling from the height
where
I have willed
an oak tree

a trio of contemplations

it began at birth

I was born

I no longer
deny it

it was an act
of air
and exposure

a fact
of reflection
on the likelihood
that

>*here I am*

on the act of

>*no other way*

I was born
and there *I*
turned into me

it happened
and from there
to now
I am

~

not ephemeral

it is only real
because it lasts
you see

what good sense
lies in a thing
that is ephemeral . . .

gone
before you were aware of it
before you saw it

only recognised
by the haze left
after a passing moment

that isn't real

but
when you cast your mind . . .

cast the focus
of your inner eye
to see the story

how one moment
becomes another
before it fades

and as you watch
that particular of time
unfold
you somehow know
that what has happened —
in the heart of you
in the endurance
of one moment
with another moment —

that becomes the story
you can tell

~

memory of moments

memory
is the assembler
of moments

idle things that
one-on-one
become a thing that happened

your story

in *your* moments

remembered
in a sequence
that seems *something like*
what happened
if
you've remembered it
right

cherishing

and I
am cherishing

> the soft sounds
> of traffic on the road
>
> a bright sheen of sunlight
> reflecting from the plum tree
> into my eyes
>
> the magpie song
>
> the autumn lushness
> of vegetables
> not yet turned
> by season change
> by cold and frost
> from verdant green
>
> the stillness
> of air and light
> hovering
> breath withheld
> above the garden

while I gaze
beyond the aroma of my coffee

cherishing

pretty day

what a day

what a pretty day

the sun is gleaming . . .

everything

there is ash
in the fire-pit
where we sat last night

I drank my toast
to you
and you
to me

now
I raise my cup
of memory
again

what a pretty day

victory (over hornets)

I will take
courage in my hand
and I will weave it
into an armour
to drape
across my shoulders
and to cover
arms and legs

I will take
the earnest of my endeavour
and I will beat it
until it fits my head
a helmet
through which to see my goal

I will be suited
in a cloth
cut for my purpose

out I go
to face the enemy
airborne

I know the place —
the location of their lair

my shovel
I will anoint
not with oil
but *special powder*

>
> *hold my nerve*
>
> *move stealthy*
>
> *catch and hold*
> *my rasping breath*
>
> *brace with all my body*

I will
BANG!
the shovel down
over the tunnel mouth

fling my magic powder
deep inside

then run

before the boiling
of yellow black and lethal
rises up
to see which way
I have fled

run run

the better part of valour
is not chivalry
but
the safety
of a door
between us

    I am victory

    I am nemesis

    I am trouble
    for the sting that never rests
    in my back yard

    that tries to enter
    into my kitchen

    yah yah

    I am victory

inside

what is the inside
of a poem

>   are you there
>   if you live it

>   do you have to know
>   or is it
>   anyway

~

what is the inside
of your life

>   do you reside
>   in stanzas

>   must you recite yourself
>   or are you
>   because you

~

your image has
a lyric flow

your life is rhythm
rhyme

your world
a driven cadence

how is it
living on the inner side

come read to me

your life
in time

creative space

everybody tells me
I've got holes
inside my head

I say

no

> they're just
> sinuses

> no
> that's space
> around the cortex
> of me

they tell me
that I'm wrong

that I've got emptiness
in the places
where my thinking
should get done
but I say

no

> that's just
> silence

> no
> that's the place
> where my thoughts
> grow
> and turn themselves
> into my big ideas

they laugh at me

say
I've got nothing
there

but I tell them

no

> *that's the place*
> *where genius*
> *will show*
>
> *and anyway . . .*
>
> *and anyway . . .*
>
> *I have nothing more*
> *to say to you*
> *just now*
>
> *I'm busy*
> *thinking*

dark substance

there is a sleep
that comes
as night-time weaves
around you

patterns moving
speckled light
against the black

shadow substance
that tears away
before your hands
if you reach
to touch it

wraps —
inside the dream —
a still-shaped form
of you

patterns move
and the play unfolds

contorted situations
show as real

but it's only night-time
weaving
the speckle-dark

insubstantial
as the dust
of what you have dreamt
before

waiting westerly

the wind raises its intensity
before a change
that is full of weather

I am lying in the darkness
waiting
for the rain

the stars I watch
through a window
are swallowed
by slow cloud
and leave nothing
but the restlessness
of leaves

like me
they are waiting
the weather
westerly

what day is this

the day
is not long
but
my boredom
makes it longer

impatient
I with the this and the that
of my lot
I cannot bear
to bother

and time drags
on me

the day
is not short
but
my excitement
makes the minutes heighten

and before I know . . .

hours have flown

the day
is a day
but —
in my mood —
I shape it

> *into more*
> *into less*
> *into nothing at all*
> *into forever*

this is my day
what
will it be

what is, if it won't

what is time
if it will not last
for me

what a waste —
in the end —
I can't hold it

what is time —
to me —
if it is so
fleeting

if I take a moment
only to find
it is gone

what is time
without a little body

it is a spectre
that holds everything

that I am

everything that I was

what is time . . .

how long do I have
to tell you

all that I know
about time
is already gone

the drafter

he draws words
like paint shaped on canvas

tiny brush strokes
of language

stories
spun from flax
stories
spun out of gold

an alphabet
hued in colour
like the leaf
green then yellow
to wine
then to earth
onto earth
into earth

there is a word . . .

call it
drafting

a journey-tool
of lettered precision

he carves the mark
that is himself
into strokes
and curls
and dashes

until the peace
that is the falling of the sun
descends upon him
loudly in the evening

he finds he doesn't know
what was sentence
what was shading

he gifts it to you
the picture
with its brush-pattern words

to you
to seek the meaning
in the work
of a draft-shapen
man

so handsome (what a guy)

oh!
mister red
you are beautiful

oh yes you are

oh mister red
you are so handsome
I know

it is true

oh mister red
I think
I love you

mmm hmmm

mmm hmmm

it is the first of may
autumn is being pushed by the passage of days
towards winter

the scarlet robin has materialised
in full colour
red chest
black wings
white diamond across the back

perky
full of bounce
delighted with himself

he has found the side mirror
on my car

and is leap-flying
up and down
in an overt self-admiration

> *you are beautiful*
> *mister red*
>
> *ooohhh!*
> *aren't you handsome*
>
> *mister red*
>
> *I think*
>
> *I really think*
>
> *you're so dashing*
> *mister red*
>
> *ooo-ooohhh!*
> *mister red*

an hour has passed
the robin has gone away

but
only for moments

the image

that so-attractive image
has dragged him back
time and again

who
could ever have enough
of a sight
so handsome

> *ooohhh*
> *mister red!*

in jerusalem

I will accept
the old borders

    jerusalem

turn me back
to the way I was

I will go forward
my dreams are of
jerusalem

where I stand
is where
I must be

    jerusalem

    jerusalem

how I crave to be
in jerusalem

I am not brave

I cannot fight

I will not wear the bullets
of desire
but . . .

    jerusalem

my heart is waiting
to stand
with you

    in jerusalem

crescent tonight

I see you
shining
you old crescent moon

a sliver you were
just last night

now you are bright
in your lemon shading

emerging
cheshire like

I see you shine
while the world hangs black
around you

crescent moon
you inspire me

a light suggestion
where darkness rules

I will see you
tomorrow

I will see you
the next night too

I will watch you growing

and brightening
the sky of night

crescent moon

for me

I entice the water
to come down

there is a cloud up there
full laden

I stand beneath
and do a dance
end with my hands up
pleading

    come down

I make a gesture

    come down

I *hither*
with my hands

    come down

the rain stays up there
just as it started
but . . .

I entice the water
with my dance

and
I entice
the water with my movement

yes
I entice as though
I am so sure

but the water . . .

no no

the water

uh-ahhh

the water . . .

no it won't
come down

not for me

three faces in a car

the first
was a sudden dog
a small
white-faced thing
with a hanging fringe
of ears

attentive black eyes
interpreting
everything that passed
on the street

every movement

the second face was
a partial man
with half his head
hidden behind
the white of the dog
in front

a passenger —
in the passenger seat —
seeing the head of the dog
from behind

seeing nothing

hearing the news
translated
second-paw

gazing intently
at white fur
through thick eye-glasses

the third . . .

well
I don't know
maybe I just imagined it

a corona

an aura

a halo light
shining three deep
and an edge wider
than that same passenger seat

filtering the spirit world
of coffee and cake
and chatter
and wasp life

a cigarette smoked

welcome to earth
welcome to latte street
welcome . . .

here comes the driver
now

humming

here am I
humming
as though singing a sing

    hi-ay-ay-ay
    ay-aii
    a-hi-hi-hi-ii

it is evening
I am making a tune
in my mind
over-
flowing
like music
into my

    ai-ay-ay-aiy

    hoo-hoo-hoo-oo

it's just like
a so-ong

like sing-i-i-ii-i-ing

    boo-
    boo-boo-boo-boo-boo-oo

I
I-I am humming a song

    mmm-hmmm-mmm

just chili (not dangerous)

well
burn my mouth
you can't frighten me
you old leather

dry you in the air
I crush you
taste
only in sprinkles

call you *jalapeño* (no no)
call you *cayenne* (uh uh)
call you
nothing much at all

you're no *bishop's crown*
you are no
ghost scorpion
(*bhut jolokia*)

yes
yes-yes I've got respect
but no
you are an ordinary
not dangerous

just an *ordinary*

that's all that's all

that is all

friend (no friend) at the door

that old wasp
is back
at my glass door

knocking with her head
trying to gain entry

    why

I am no friend to wasps

    why

is it a journey
to take vengeance
on me

that old wasp
in inside my house

not really
but . . .

there it is
a shape flying
in shadow
across the floor

using the sun to help

projecting it's presence
through the glass

    oh my oh my

that old wasp
is back in my thoughts
butting her head
up against me

this is a vengeance wrought

> *knock knock*
> *knock knock*

that old wasp
is not a friend
of mine

in the day

the muted light
of six ay-em

the stillness . . .

    new morning

a quiet burble-song

    the magpie calls
    the day

and a wash of sound
is a car afloat
on the tarmac lined
street canyon

eyes open

eyes waken

    here it comes
    again

eyes open
eyes waken
and here it comes
again

and here
I am

sleepy

the morning sleeps
late

I will not wake her

the sun has risen
long ago
in silence
to not disturb

the birds hop quiet
and whisper chatterings

and the blue —
like a blanket —
sings warm

sleep deep
sleep long

the day will still be day
when you awaken

time
will allow
in its long reckoning

sleep sweet
morning

a sleepy song

fly

oh the days
fly by

like confetti leaves
leaping from the safe embrace
of autumn trees
into the twirl and swirl
the crease and curl
that is *winter*
soon

first the colour . . .

then let go

>*goodbye*
>*goodbye*

they fly

security
safety . . .

that is for spring

for summertime
and growing

but now . . .

a second chance
while the whistle-wind
begins to howl

wear a party frock

wear a scarf

some trinkets

discard the veil

kiss the tree

kiss the tree of home
and fly

a pattern

I feel
the pattern of the rain
as dark drops
spreading into each other
across the pavement

I feel it
revealed
in the tattoo
on my rooftop now

the colour
is every colour
made richer
at a touch

the pallet
drawn from an endless sea
uniformly grey

the texture
is a sound
that lulls my mind
to sleep
in a blanket
tugged higher
in the middle of a dream

of rainy nights
when raindrops rebound
back into the air
only to fall —
a sigh —
again

words like a painters oils

each word
is like a touch
of painters oil
colour chosen
from the palette

a stroke of brightness
daubed *just there*
a blend

the shape
emergent

and as the brushwork
finds its pace
each touch and daub
and stroking
a picture —
the picture —
unremarked at first . . .

unfurls
to be seen
for what it shows

these words . . .

they are a picture

> *read one line*
> *then close your eyes*
>
> *watch the scene*
> *that has been whispered*
> *into your mind*

like painters' oil
applied to white paper

fly high prayer

high cloud

a wisp
and a trail of white

low cloud

billow
boil
cotton fluff swirl-around

like milk
in my coffee

prayer flags
in a flock
of *wheel-and-turn*
flutter white
under the sun

a pigeon prayer
for gentle days
like this one

high fly
wisp yourself
away from me

while I
wheel and turn
pour milk
into my latte

billow
a prayer to you

flag
and wave
the sun

heaven glimpsed (leaves down)

oak tree
time has come

let your leaves fall down

oak tree
their green is gone

let your leaves
fall down

I see the sky up there

glimpse heaven
through your fingers

open up
to the blue

and
let your leaves
come down

deep breathing

fire in the heater

footy on the box

chilling in the lounge
with my legs up

it is a reclining chair
and I
am fully laid-back

look outside
the window
shows rain
transformed to sleet now . . .

to snow
blowing around
like leaves
down from their autumn trees

I took the lid off
the red wine

I like it better
when it has a chance
to do some breathing

like me

a sunday afternoon
and I am
lying back and just
deep breathing

Winter 2017

winter oh

oh
oh oh winter

you come with a sky
full of stars
the ground paved in frost

in icicles

you mist my mouth
while I am trying to breathe

I feel you
in my bones . . .

the way that my face
tries so hard
not to ache
and fails

wintertime

I should have known
when the robin came
that you
would be close behind

the clarity
of your nights is a deception

it is just a blanket
of you

frozen air

oh winter
you are come
and I feel you
deep
in me

I am cold

time is up

I can hear
the coffee grind
coming from the kitchen

I'm a lazy old fool
who is still in bed

even though
the blue is up
and the yellow down

even though
the magpie outside
is wardle-ing

> *why*
> *aren't you up*
>
> *why are you*
> *still sleeping*
>
> *come on come on*
> *the day is awake*
> *and calling*

I no longer hear
the coffee being ground
in the kitchen

it is time
and I
am rising

season to season

the yellows
and the oranges
and the reds
of the fallen

overtaken by brown

overtaken by the earth

covered over
by the white

and the season creeps along
hiding green
deep
beneath the grey
of fog
and the following
reflected gleams of light
from the sun

low
but shining

trench man #1: the trench man's tools

see them at rest

they are embracing
like weary comrades

they have dug
straight
and dug deep
and they are weary

can you see —
in the lost space —
the shape
of an absent digger . . .

one leg knee deep
the other bent
beneath him

first
the mattock
wielded
then the trenching
by spade

begun in the morning
as just an idea

pushed through
to lunchtime
it is a line

deep
into evening
the trench
has been opened

trench-man
can rest
and his tools
embrace

trench man #2: almost (so far to go)

well
he took his tools
in the soft
morning light

broke through
soil
and clay

cleared the dirt
from the straight
true line

and bent his back
as though praying
to the gods
of *digging a line*

when he looked
how far

      (*not far enough*)

when he looked
how far

      (*so far still to go*)

he looked at his hands
and they wept for him
but . . .

the mattock knows now
the way he likes to strike

the shovel fits snug
to his grasp

and they swing
and they clear —
with the end in sight —
and they know
they are almost . . .

almost
they are almost home

trench man #3: to the end or until

the tools grow heavy
his arms so weak
the loose dirt wobbles
like a jelly
on the spoon

he thinks
he ought to widen this trench
to take his shoulders
and his head
let it taper down
to his feet

before it is dug
he might be wanting both
a coffin
and a grave

he can see the finish now —
nearer —
but there's so much
still to do

the clay
clings
like a cloying lover
too long on the spade
but
there's nothing he can do about it

just swing down
again

clear the debris
and inch by inch
to the end
or until
his punishment stops

trench man #4: home before texture

he comes to know
the feel of clay

gets the *taste*
by smelling it

not a potter
but
he slices clean
and smooth
with the keen blade
of his shovel

so many strata

> *green*
> *then dirt*
> *to ochre-orange*
>
> *brown*
> *into death-white*

a whole palette uncovered
before he meets the depth
he is aiming for

perhaps he should
while away a little time
by testing texture
in his hand

but no . . .

there is just a metre
to go

always
there is just another metre
to go
before home

trench man #5: the nature of the job

his job
is the creation
of absence

each shovel filled
is a movement
into
negative space

the measure
of his work
is the quality
of removal

> *straight walls*
>
> *level floor*
>
> *just so*
> *high*
>
> *just so*
> *wide*

all of it filled —
through his diligence —
with nothing

trench man #6: foreign substance

the brick
is a foreign substance

where the trench runs
straight
and true
the brick
is a deviation

it can't be sliced
with a shovel

it can't be scraped away
without ruining
the line

the brick
is not of *this* earth

it should not be here

bend the line . . .

gouge or excavate
a hole . . .

the brick –
either way –
is nothing but trouble

it should not
be here

trench man #7: staggered end

another blow struck
and he staggers
as the blade
passes through

part exhaustion
part relief
he stares
at what he has exposed

nowhere
to nowhere

just a line
of emptiness
etched into the ground

.

.

.

another day

one *other* day

he will start
at one end

to turn the clods
the clay and soil
and bricks
back

so the proof
he was here
might never
be found

trench man #8: to achieve the cool

then the tradie comes along
while he is taking a blow
squatting in his own shadow
on wet ground

> *mighty fine work*

the tradie says

> *yes*
> *it's mighty fine*
> *but*

another six inches
to get close
to the depth

six inches down
or
a mile

it seems
all much the same
to the mattock
and the spade

and there is nothing to do
but go deeper
and know that
one of these days . . .

sometime soon . . .

he will be out of this slush

sometime soon
he will be done

but for the moment . . .

for tonight . . .

there will be a beer
in the fridge

and it will chill
to power
that he has dug
under the ground

and the trench he is in now —
up to his knees —
will be a part of that cool
so it's
get on
and dig

like a rabbit

dig
like a fool

trench as though
it will be finished . . .

one of these days
and
some time

soon

closing time

the sky
is visible
through the oak tree

that old friend of mine
is closing down
for the season

I can see now
the companion birds
so well hidden
in the days
of green

so small as they flitter
among falling leaves
adrift on a cool breeze
that has come
from a *somewhere*
cradling snow

for it kisses my face
with the tender love
of a wintry slap

and the sun
has no strength
to do more
than glow now

the clouds are visible
through my oak tree

that old friend of mine
is closing down
for the cold

might as well

every absence
is a loneliness

every loneliness
is an idea
of *forever*

and people
all around
people
everywhere
people

nothing there

the sun shines down
sol
up there
by himself

watching the moon
watching the stars
watching earth

looking down at me

too bright
I don't see him
only the yellow-white
of his glare

too bright
I wonder
if anyone ever sees
what is there

near enough to warm
too far away
to touch
he might as well
be here

go and pick (ordering alliums)

who
will go and pick
three alliums

thick and lush . . .

they are
so young

>   *onion*
>   *leek*
>   *sativa bulb*

who will pick
that I might eat

.

.

.

will no one
brave
these three alliums

they are strong
but . . .

be not weak

three stalk leaves
and one fine bulb

who'll bring flavour
for my feed

.

.

.

must *I* go
to pick three alliums

they are forest
like to trees

tough and hard
and garlic strong

must I go
to get my peace

.

.

.

is there truly
no one
to rid me

of these paltry
alliums

they are but onions
do you not see

bitter
weeping
grow some skin

who will brave
alliums
for me

shush-ing the oak tree

shu-shu-shush

the oak tree
is dreaming

shu-shu-shush

his leaves
are all leaving

shu-shu-shush

he is not paying attention
to you
or to me

shu-shu-shush

maybe he is listening

shu-shu-shush

let's sing . . .

he might hear us

shu-shu-shush

let's *shu-shu-shu-shu*
shuffle his music
along

shu-shu-shush

let's shuffle his music
in this song

hoary hoary

all through the night
I whiten you

all in the dark
I am the light

in you
and out

    hoary hoary

crystal and diamond

sun
ha!

I make you shine

    hoary hoary

old bastard I
pretty in blue

I
pretty
you

whistle if

whistle if you think

ba-ba-ba-baba

whistle if you feel

ba-ba-ba-baba

whistle if you think
and
whistle if you feel

whistle if you

be-ba-ba-ba-baaa

doo-do-doo-do-do

doo-do-do-do

and

doo-do-doo-do-do

doo-do-do-do

dee-dat-dat-dat-da-da-dada
dee-dat-da-da-da-daaaaa

da-da-da-dada daaa-daaa
da-da-dada-da-daaaa

whistle if feel like

oh yeah

whistle if you feel like

yeah ye-yeah

whistle if you feel that
welling up inside

whistle if you feel
you have to

      baaaaaaaa
      ba

      baaaaaaaa
      ba-ba
      baaaaaaaa

last remains

a graveyard
of brown

a nudity
of oak

the grey sky
above
has loomed low

with a chill breath
it blows
last leaves
away from home

the branches
in their lichen
the last remains

stripping

beneath the paint
the timber
resides

mountain ash
that once grew . . .

oh
so tall

so straight

in the heart
of the rain forest

length by length
painted
canary bright

used to seat the children
swimming
in municipal pools

beneath the paint —
still pure —
the heartwood

in dabs and blobs
a coating applied
of a *jelli-um*

something
derived
from something else

wait and watch . . .

from the cracks
the bubbles rise
soaking deep
while lifting

I feel the burn
seep into —
across —
my fingers

this is not sport
it is a fire
of redemption

and as the scraper
ploughs
and digs
yellow ribbons
curl above the sludge
and fly
off to the side

away to ground

and where the paint
is pushed away
it reveals
the pallor —
like skin
cloistered beneath a parasol —
of the wood

the straight grained wood
is revealed again

I would not have thought
to be so moved
by this
rescue
and revelation

but when the garish
yellow
is gone
what is left
is the purity
of mountains

once a hole

he is
a prisoner

the poet prisoner

his jailer
laughs

> *what will you write*
>
> .
> .
> .
>
> *of this*
>
> *a ha ha*
>
> *and what*
> *will you make.*
>
> .
> .
>
> *out of that*

blood spills

droplets
to the floor

teeth fall
hardly a sound
where they settle

each movement

each moment

brings him close
to the end

.
.
.

a gift of paper
small
a gift of pencil
blunted to stub

> *come*
> *come*
>
> *come you poet*
> *write me your poem*
> *write me*
> *now*

~

the universe is black
and contained
within a room

four rising walls
and a hardened floor

there are no openings

only
the dark

until . . .

the beam of a lonely ray
up in a roof

so high up
he can hardly
imagine it

the sun
is a kindness
with a benevolent face
who longs to shine
even into dark places
where no welcome lingers
to greet passing light

a single ray
through an unguessed hole

a halo
around a sharp white point

first
high on a wall
then slow-moving around
and down

circling the room

lower
low
towards the floor

as daytime passes
and the sun moves
in its progression

through the sky

slowly
so so slow

until ray meets floor
and shines its light
for a moment in passing
upon the upturned face
of one poor man

on his knees

face upturned
eyes closed

reverent as
a worshipper

praising
the sun

~

    so

    so you poet
    mine

    so that is a poem

    well
    I know it now

    I know you now

    tomorrow I will pound a poem
    of my own
    metal on metal

    can you guess the name
    my poem will be called

    once
    a hole
    was here

    a-ha
    a ha ha ha

    once
    was a hole

***oonga boonga* (power to the people)**

the government wants to charge me
for the electricity
I make

I have a power plant
sun-worshipping
on my rooftop

even though
I make it for myself
the government
wants to take it

they don't want to build
their own power plant

    oh no no no

they don't want
to be touched
by dirty coal

    oh no no no

they love the sun

    oh yes yes yes

they love
my
sun

    oh yes yes yes yes

they pay me peanuts
for power

they pay me
enough so I can't say

    it's nothing

now they want to charge me
a small premium

    oh no no no

a little extra something
I've never before
had to pay

    oh no no no

when will it end

    no never ever

will they never leave us
to try to support the earth

    she is dying all the time

I think
I'll go back
to the stone age

    oonga boonga

think I'll just
regress

    ka boonga

sometimes
I can't wait
for the end

it's surely coming

the end

surely coming

sure

Frank Prem

the school cleaner

he arms himself
on a daily basis
with the tools required
by his trade

> *a broom —*
> *of course —*
> *and a mop and bucket*
>
> *solvent*
> *and a three-inch paintbrush*
>
> *a duster*
> *an eraser*
>
> *assorted cloths*
>
> *a chisel*
> *he has sometimes found useful*
>
> *and a hammer*
>
> *some weights*
>
> *protective clothing*
> *(obviously)*
>
> *overalls*
> *dark glasses*
> *heavy boots*
> *rubber gloves*
>
> *a helmet*
> *because . . .*
>
> *well you never could tell*

enough

enough to make a start
to the working evening

he finds that each room
has a different
flavour

the beginner's rooms
are just a mess

> *loose letters*
> *naïve words*
>
> *singletons*
>
> *half formed couplets*

strewn and abandoned
on the floor
in corners
under the desks

simple enough
to sweep them up
into a seething mess
then scoop them
into recycling

the more advanced rooms
though
spell trouble

ha ha
not a pun

some of those phrases
can be curly

> *almost as fully complete*
> *as meaningful stanzas*
> *before the sense of them*
> *has flown*
> *leaving despair and resentment*
> *trailing in black lines*
> *of entrapment*

he might have to stop these
in their tracks

possibly whack down
leading lines with the hammer

>   *glove up*

>   *handle carefully*

words can sometimes
do a lot of harm

and the 'S' room
is a shocker

all those sibilants
curling round everything
seeming alive

and slippery

he can show no mercy there

almost as disturbing
as having to contain
the over-friendly 'T's next door

sometimes
an unpleasant student
will scribble
or carve
on the furniture

some small doggerel
but *always*
with a nasty bite

out with the solvent
or the stripper

hammer and chisel
if it is extreme

but the teachers
might be
the worst

the rubbish they leave
on blackboards

on whiteboards

the gifted ones let their nonsense
linger
in the air

left there for him
to clean up after them

left for him
to leave things gleaming

unsullied
by mis-formed rhyme
or
an absence of free-verse

no pentameters
no sonnets

he gets paid
peanuts for it

not enough to compensate
for the nightmares
of letters and words running
through his mind

not enough
for the loss of sleep

and they say
that *HE*
has no imagination

ho ho
bloody ho

he's half a mind
to chuck this job

words and all

he kicks
at the loose middle third
of an alphabet

shoves the last letters
into a plastic garbage bag
for incineration
and he's done

off home now
for a drink

five bird poems (benalla)

highway (crows)

crows shine
on the shoulder
of the highway

stride —
business like —
from carrion to carrion

ruffs alert to the tender kiss
of a passing breeze

black feet
black beak
black feathers

black crows
shine
on the shoulder
of the highway

~

evaluation of a swimmer

the line of wake
is a duck
is a dabchick

a moorhen

the bobbing of her head
is the forcing rhythm
of hard work
under water

a flotilla of ducks —
sedate —
by the shore
consider their evaluation

but a quack
is such a nasal thing
that
whatever their conclusion
I'll never know

~

slow water (cockatoo-ing)

lazy river
upside down

your silt rides
on the surface

making
a turbulent mirror
for the sun
to reflect an arc
of cockatoos
in slow flight

sky
among the branches
of a restless corrugation
raised
by soft breeze
soughing low
along the rippling water line

but hardly touching
red gum leaves
that dangle close
and lazy

slow river
slow waves
slow
slow water

~

cockatoo tree

a cockatoo tree

white
against olive

the afternoon —
this afternoon —
is for sleeping

until you wake up
a hundred . . .

one hundred pairs
of wings
flapping
to cockatoo a sky
full of squawking

cockatoo

your white
against
the stainless blue

~

dabbler

moor hens
on the foreshore

dabchicks
on the grass

red faced
red chased
by other moor hens

dabbling the river

and still
it rolls

currawong cries

    koo-warr-koo-warr-koo-warr-ka
    koo-warr-koo-warr-koo-warr-ka

my mother told me
they cawed and called
and gathered
in their groups
just before rain

    koo-warr-koo-warr-koo-warr-ka
    koo-warr-koo-warr-koo-warr-ka

she said
they were an infallible
indicator

but I believe . . .

    koo-waa-aa-arrrrhh

I believe

    waa-aa-aa-aa- arrrrhh

she was wrong

the big bird
at the top of the tree
is alone

she is looking out
but she isn't watching
for the weather

    koo-warr-koo-warr-koo-warr-ka

my currawong stares
away to the east

if she sees weather coming
she will not tell me

    koo-waa-aa-arrrrhh

I think she is just bored

maybe
in-between jobs

or waiting till the rest
of the criers arrive
for the corroboree

    koo-warr-koo-warr-koo-warr-ka
    koo-warr-koo-warr-koo-warr-ka

    koo-waa-aa-arrrrhh

    koo-warr-koo-warr-koo-warr-ka
    koo-warr-koo-warr-koo-warr-ka

    waa-aa-aa-aa- arrrrhh

the morning rings
the mourning cries

the currawongs
are carrion the dead

    waa-aa

the currawongs
are singing

    waa-aa-aa-aa- arrrrhh

for the dead

still (day) life

the silence of the day
hangs
waiting in the light
of a desultory sun

this is winter

the leaves have fallen
down

tree skeletons
are pointed
up

there is not a breath
of wind

yet . . .

it is peaceful

the clouds lack energy enough
to hold together

they have spread themselves
out
across the sky

the birds have no news
to chortle

the day
is a completely still life

in its way
artistic

a waking wind

in the dead
of night
the sleeper wakes
to the whistling wind

    woo woo-woo

returned
from a journey
to antarctica

    woo woo-woo

sleep on

in the soft light
of a new day —
grey —
the sleeper wakes
to a pattering

    woo woo-woo

rain has come
dragged behind the flaring skirt
of a moaning wind

    woo woo-woo

sleep on

sleep on

at brunetti's

there is a sparrow
in brunetti's
on a fly-by

but the cakes
are locked away

the tables
are free of crumbs

even children
chase any morsel
that might get away

profiterole mountains
are like buddha's
chocolate coated child

and birthday greetings
are a flowery script
swirled
onto white chocolate slabs
for a party
and *to go*

the coffee
is as black
as night

I think I see
the future
in bubbled runes
that coat the side
of my bespoken cup

it tells me
I will be back
tomorrow

for your (brunetti) birthday

brunetti's
home deliver your birthday

bundled
in a cake box
held —
gently —
by a ribbon
in a bow

the italian
sharp young man
fires up his vespa

wheels away
to greet you —
a little swagger —
at your door

random city

the cityscape
in high rise jumble

is the superstructure
of an ocean liner

sailing

too big to turn

~

black tights
and heels

black crows
in groups
and squabbles

I have never seen
so many
in just one place

puppet show: the foyer

munchkin little children
in arms

on the floor

mothers
engaged
before the show

men standing around
in pork pie hats
flat caps
and pointed noses

dust motes
rise and dance
in the warmth
of a downlight
that reveals us
all

museum #1 – the museum jungle

the cacophony
of a jungle

I am in amongst
dinosaurs

and the taxi-dermeevery-creature
to ever move
around the planet

they are not here
it is just their bones

their skin

but children
are squeal-and-calling
in their hundreds

I turn
to the hunting-posed lion
beside me
catch his eye

both of us think

    pray

museum #2 – in the trenches

in the wartime dioramas
the walls
remodel themselves
as you move

woodlands green
transformed
out of pock-mud graves
and corpses

rolling
nineteen fifteen
into today
seamlessly enough
to confound
your mind
and your vision

the narrow trenches
of *world war one*
are clogged
by the mass of bodies

of museum soldiers

and war is hell
when the only way out
is blocked

jammed

solidified

by a mother
with a four-wheel-drive
perambulator

we are all
going to die
here

museum #3 – the whale

(pigmy blue whale)

wey-hey wey-hey
I am looking in the mouth
of a whale

I will surrender myself –
his baleen
to my krill –

filter and wash me
clean
never again
to be seen

wey-hey wey-hey
looking down the barrel
of the whale

fending

the ristorante
shuts down
sometime
in the early hours

tables and chairs
taken in from the street
overhead gas fires
turned down
turned out

all that remains
is a sidewalk corral
and the stiff plastic sheeting
that keeps away
the road
stops the weather

in the morning light
there is a body
in a swag
with a letter —
on the beg —
beside it

life treasures
in a supermarket trolley
in the inside corner

a good long sleep
restores the body

shelter
from the storm

another day begins
fending off
the street

victorian war memorial 070717

every soldier's face
is the same face

he is young
he is blond
he stands straight
in a uniform
that fits him well

sometimes
he is in the navy

he looks
an australian

perhaps it's his slouch hat . . .

perhaps the way
the cap is perched

he is
a serious young man
gazing at his future
somewhere
just off to one side
of the camera

he is smoking
a cigarette
with his mates

he is the statue
of himself
placed back-to-back

he is gone now

he is always
here

faux song in the city

he awakened
to the rain

steady rain
falling and falling

>*a constant*
>*strong*
>*patter*

only with the slow rise
of awareness
came the realization

>*he is not*
>*at home*
>*beneath a tin roof*
>*but in a hotel*
>*in the city*
>
>*on the first floor*

through the window
he saw the source
of his not-rain

>*air conditioners*
>*humming*
>*rattling*
>*in a constant patter*
>*of sound*

an auditory imitation
of home

veil dance (oh no)

it is a dance of veils
in the fireplace
at night

heat
has separated the bark
from the wood
of a log that I have thrown
onto the hearth

flickering tongues
of yellow and blue
are appearing

    (lick)

disappearing

twirling as though
they are arms raised
sinuously

    (lick)

then . . .

disappearing

the bark —
as it lifts
so slowly away —
is a checkerboard
of burn

coloured —
very slightly
volcano—

very slightly alive

and it is throbbing

    (lick)

oh no

    (lick)

oh no no no

home to the swirling
gyring
of hunger

home
to the voluptuous *oh no*
no no

    (lick)

no no no

no
no no no

burning acrobats
performing in the fire

conflagrating
a veil mirage
that is all shimmer *oh no*

oscillation scintillation
glimmer into gleam

    (lick)

oh no
oh no

the fire
no no
is dancing flames

distorting light
around the burn
in the heart
oh no
no no no
no no no

it is the dance
of fire and veils

it is the dance

new coffee

the beans bleed
like chocolate blood

suddenly

through the spout
of the percolator

as though a vein —
cut
has released
all that it holds —
it pours
up
while the heat below it
drives

until a gurgling
empty sound

the death throes
of a crush
of freshly roasted beans
signals
they have given
all they have got

go
drink it

go sip go sup
go high —
just a little —
on the smell
of new coffee

the magpie song

I am w-*ordle-ordle*-alking
the sun
is on my back
and I speak softly
to the

    HEY-HEY-HEY-HEY

w-*ordle-ordle*
ordle-orms
hoping they might rise
and sing this

    HEY-HEY-HEY-HEY
    HEY

s-*ordle*-ong
with me

it is lovely
in this

    HEY-HEY-HEY

sunshine

I still h-*ordle-ordle*-ope
the w-*ordle*-orms might
sing al-*ordle-ordle*-ong

there is beauty
in this

    HEY-HEY-HEY-HEY

day

wordle-ordle

how it begins

it begins
with a roiling
of the clouds

> *deep grey*
> *spinning on itself*

> *light grey cast*
> *streaking*
> *the sky*

it begins
with the troubling
of the limbs
of a winter eucalypt

> *swaying sprays*
> *in agitation*

> *while a setting sun*
> *golds the canopy*
> *as though denial*
> *is so easily won*

it begins
with the restless relocation
of fallen autumn leaves

> *most already gone*
> *into earth dreaming*
> *but the few that remain*
> *sleep troubled*
> *and move*
> *across the ground*

it begins
with a *woo-ing*
of the wind

*streaking past them all
raising tensions high
flying past
again*

the trembling grasses
know
it has begun

the sleeping oak
is aware
it has begun

collage (ti-ri-ol)

    ti-ri-ol

the sky
so grey
it is white now

    ti-ri-ol

the tree so bare
is black
silhouetted
against the sky
so white

    ti-ri-ol

the green
around the tree base
is flecked with brown

becoming black tree

a silhouette
against
the white

    ti-ri-ol

the magpie
walks the green
foraging
in the brown
becomes the singer
of the black tree

    ti-ri-ol

against the white

ti-ri-ol

the grey
still
is in the sky

ibis to land

the undercarriage
of an ibis
descending
is a hang glider
with its legs out
already searching for the *firma*
from high up
and circling
a little unsteadily
circling
a line between
trees
above shrubs
and the fence
to land

to land
nonchalant

a few strides

sog descending

there is a mist
from the west
blowing over the fence
in fine waves

abandoning
the neighbour's house

it drives
like the wind is behind it
though it's still
outside

a dampened quiet

last night
I lay awake
to the sound of rain
in downpour

in droplets

like wet blows
struck upon the tin
by a tympanic hammer

with all else
asleep
struck specially
for my ear

it has turned
to fog now

a sog

closing in
and taking the tall trees
out of my sight

though I know
they are still there

.
.
.

I believe
they are still
right
there

cling-wrap the day

there is nothing
else
to do

the air-craft of kitchen utensils

father to son
a gifting
of skills

all down the line

here
a set of knives
sharpened on the wind

singing
knife songs
to the clouds

seeking the right pitch
to slice
right through the breeze

there
four flat plates
transparent clear

packed dense
to hold a meal
of substance

perhaps a steak

a roast potato

floating
as though nothing
holds them underneath

unravelled
with a blow
of warm air
from your mouth

no need to wash them
no earthly need
to store

just let them go

just
let them blow

into the element
from which they came

let them blow

father
to son

a gifting of skills

useful utensils
whistled
from the air

empty starlings

empty tree

one starling

empty tree

two starlings

I look away
I look again

I look away
I look again

at an empty tree

two starlings

empty tree

three starlings

I look away
I look again

I look away
I look again

at an empty tree

three starlings

empty tree

four starlings

Winter 2017

I look away
I look again

at an empty tree

five

the hunt for the wild arancini

the wild arancini
gallops
across the driving range

the golf club chef —
so close behind him —
holds his implements
up high

his cook's knife

the roasting fork

a sharpening steel
held to his wrist
by a shortened length
of cord

the apron flies
a-flap
around his knees

his moustache
is beaded sweat
while his jowls
are in full motion
in broad wobble

but he runs
full stretch
as a lion
might

the prey
leaps and bounds
more like
a gazelle

across the 10th
and over the slight undulations
of a two-shot
to fairway
from tee

out of a rough lie
the chef emerges suddenly
but the arancini
is away

the chef
seeks only a small cut

a *smallest*
cut

the club president
will dine today
with guests

but
the run
of the arancini

is wild

it is wild
and will brook no trade

no portion mutilated
be it large
or small

he will remain *uncut*
until the pennant
waves

.

.

.

the chef sits
sadly
half-sprawled
across the 11th green

the only ball available
rattling —
lonely—
in the cup

alas
alas

mere batter
and poor rice —
a humble filling —
will have to serve
for this entrée

there is a bray
from the woods
that run alongside
the 14th

the arancini —
a-prance with the strut
of freedom —
now stops to graze

no backward glance

no moment
so wasted

the magnificent aperitif
drifts
almost vanishing
beyond
the back nine

harmony (minor)

if we harmonise
a minor chord

we can make the wind

> *blow-woe-woe*
> *ooo ooo*

I feel the thrum of you
deep inside me

a vibration

> *ooo-ooo*
> *woe-woe-woe-woe*
>
> *ohhhhh-ohhhh*
> *o-ohhh-ohh*

I watch you change
the shape
you are holding your mouth

you close your eyes

> *ohhh-ohh*
> *ohhh-oh-woe-woe*
> *ohhh-oh*
> *woe-wo*   *ooh-oooh*

I watch you

> *oooh-oooh*

we harmonise
the wind

in a minor third

Frank Prem

the name on the grave 'who am I'

who am I

>I prayed
>as I knew
>that I should pray
>through all the hours
>of the day
>
>I was there
>when you had need
>of me
>
>I bore
>and I raised
>with respect for you
>and for god
>
>and with love
>
>I concealed my face
>looked out
>only from shadows
>
>and I remained
>within
>
>none knew me
>without
>
>once
>I was a daughter
>
>once
>a sister
>
>once me
>
>then I lived
>with you

for you

until your time

and we placed your stone
written
with your name

now I –
devout –
seek to find the way
for myself

but tell me:

how
will I be known

how will I make my claim
to joy and justice

who will know
the person
that I am

and here

how will my children
find me

how will my daughters know
where to weep
should they seek
the comfort
of their mother

did I
truly
serve so poorly

http://www.abc.net.au/news/2017-07-31/whereismyname-afghan-women-protest-to-claim-their-identities/8760666

prowling in black and white

black/white cat

take a step
take a step
take a
very little step

ack/white cat

better pause
better stop
better halt
just wait

k/white cat

hush now
shh hush
be q-
uiet

shhh

white cat

run run run run
leap high
leap fast
claws out

ite cat

too bad
no luck
leaves rustle
birds fly

too bad

    black-
    white
    cat

walk away

groucho spy-pies

the magpies
are wearing moustaches

I think
they may be in disguise

though I haven't seen any
wearing dark glasses

it isn't spring yet
but
change must be in the air

the maggies are unceasing
in their hunt for nest materials

a length of stringy-bark
fallen from a piece
of firewood
is trodden on
to hold it down
while simultaneously worked over
with a beak

in another place
dried off grass
is ripped
and torn
with the same result

I expect there must be
a secret password

a special segment
of song carolling
that means

> *pass*
> *friend*

or

> *who are you*
>
> *I have never seen
> your moustache
> before*

they make a comical
spy outfit

groucho
would be pleased

axeman: axe time

what is the axe —
with its hungry edge —
but another means
to conquer

slice by slice
the wood-round preserved
diminuendo

the axe
is unmoved
even as the chips
encircle
and surround us

ready again
if required
to deliver a blow

and in the darkness
of the garden shed
the rhythm of sleeping
is the percussive memory
of thud
upon thud
upon . . .

time between strikes
is a no-time

no change
no awareness
but waiting

time before a new strike
is a no-time
of new-time
then

and then

a blow

my axe
is a portent
a driven cut
in the making

no mood
no mind
no time
but

a blow

street echo

mellish street
has become a canyon
again

the gutters run —
gleaming —
in the rain

every car
is an urgent roar

    and its echo

from a mile away
at the low road

    and its echo

to the high
above the town

on mellish street
I hear you coming

    and your echo

from a long mile away

you

    and the echo

in the rain

a long
mile
away

a little privacy please

chase me chase me
right out of
the lounge room

chase me chase me
right out
into the rain

chase me chase me
down the road
that is a river

chase me chase me
away
and
chase me
chase me again

then
set right down
where you can do
some yoga

set right down
where the extra company
is not a strain

set right down
stretch out
and do some yoga

then
set yourself down
stretch right out
again

weather

weather

closing in
on the radar

a green-black mass
is sliding
at a rate
of seven images
in an hour

strobing from the west
to hover
right above my door

they say

it's weather

centimetre depths
of snow
that used to counted
as feet

at least two feet

I don't like
weather

in the middle of the strobe
I see yellow

an intensity
of yellow

I think that means
it gets heavy

really heavy

Winter 2017

here I am
waiting for the rain
disguised
in a strobe of weather
but I know . . .

any time now . . .

a down fall

> *look out*
> *look out*
> *for rain*
>
> *watch out for hail*
>
> *look down*
> *in case*
> *of snow*

I really dislike
such weather

strange times

my bedclothes listed
to the left
in the middle
of last night

more usually
they slip away
to the right

these are strange times

when I opened my eyes
in the darkness
I needed comfort

my hot water bottle —
softer
as the night dragged past —
remained
a warm friend

and I slept again

this morning
when I woke
in the mystery
of left-sided sheets
the house was quiet

you were gone

these are . . .

these are
strange times

sweet old song

I'm washing away the traces
of love
in the morning
find myself singing
in the shower

a sweet old song
that you and I do well
together

and I'm thinking
it may be time
to get out
that old ukulele
of mine

maybe try to tune it

then
maybe try to tune
me

maybe later

maybe
just a little later

I'll strum the tune
and you and I
can sing that song
again

breakfast

my mouth
is filled
with the butter taste

the burn-brown
crunch
of a well-done crumpet

breakfast
is in the smell
risen
from the toaster

my nose
is filled
with the acrid burn
of beans

after the pour
has left
the espresso-maker behind

breakfast
is in the *new-ground*
of coffee

in the rituals
that begin
the day

shadow march

the shadows have struck out
overland
heading from the west
on a trail that leads
from the plum tree
towards tomorrow morning

there has been no sun
for perhaps a day
or maybe
it's been a year . . .

either way
the sun is there now —
momentarily —
and the shadows
are taking their brooding shades
and hightailing

to tomorrow
where it might be better

even their darkness
comes to life
in the daylight

maybe the climate —
the warm
or the rain —
is a factor

it doesn't really matter

the shadows are lengthening
and leaving

who knows
where they will end
who knows
when they will be returning

I wish them well
it is a long stretch
from here
all the way
to
tomorrow morning

sentinel

high point
of the tree

there you are
again

sentinel
the sun
is behind you

what are you watching

>is it my backyard

>is it the neighbour's house

>is it a change
>in the weather
>a luffing breeze

magpie
at the high point
you are
elemental

my elemental

art to be light (by and by)

when the world
is setting

when the only light —
too thin —
is a line
just kissing the east

then friends speak together
quietly . . .

in whispers

and they speak of hope
in a time of fear

they paint pictures
to show
a new day may yet rise

and pen poems of love
as small beacons

their galleries
are an art
that serves
as the act of prayer

now
when the world
is in darkness
let us draw
let us write
let us say
a light
may yet come
by and by

if we look
there will be light
by and by

Winter 2017

With thanks to Arris Grace Hodge for allowing a link to her painting 'Red Dawn': https://arrisgracehodge.wordpress.com/2017/08/10/red-dawn/

asparagus spring

the asparagus
is hearing
a hopeful song

from underground
it hears the call

>*spring*
>*oh spring*
>
>*spring will come*

the aspiring
is singing
a hopeful song

into the air
it rises

>*spring*
>*oh spring*
>
>*spring is come*

I
watch the asparagus

I sing
a hopeful song

>*spring*
>*oh spring*
>*don't be long*
>*in rising*
>
>*spring*
>
>*oh spring*
>
>*come soon*

a jonquil song

hey
hey
it's jonquil day

sing spring
sing spring

hey hey
it's jonquil day

sing spring

sing spring

hey hey hey hey

hey hey hey hey

hey hey hey

hey hey hey

hey hey hey it's jonquil day
sing spring

sing spring

jonquil day

jonquil day

spring

ing

chortle magpie

chortle me magpie

a slumbering song

spring is around us
the blue
and the sky

luffing clouds
so fluffed up
and white

chortle me magpie

chortle a song

spring
is around us

wired awake

I'm in my bed
it is before first light

there is a bird I don't know
belling
outside in the dark

she has a quiet call —
not loud enough to disturb —
but here I am
eyes open
and wired awake

wondering
if the rain will come
before the bomb gets dropped

> *I'm not afraid*
> *but I think there's a chance*
> *that I might die*
> *before morning*

it's not the kind of thing
I am used to
at this time in my life

if I were a drinking man
I would keep scotch
in a bottle
by the side of my bed

the world is quiet
except for a bird I don't know
belling quietly
outside my window

> *I am not afraid*
> *but*
> *if she should stop . . .*

I wonder
how long
before it rains

I am in my bed

it is before first light
and I am wide awake
but
not loud enough
to disturb

a west side story – wagga in the park

I feel pretty
oh so pretty . . .

the army is out

sergeant major
is a one-man baton charge
backed by brass

by wind
and by reed

maria is in love
and the army plays sharps

they are not a gang
but . . .

close

the air force –
perhaps –
can play the jets

tonight tonight . . .

I think I can hear castanets
or percussion shakers going off

it's hard to see the band
from where I am sitting

I know they are under
the bandstand rotunda
and I have clear vision
but
they are blending
into the pavilion
in camouflage fatigues
and by general stealth

only the luffing of air
as it kisses the microphones
points me towards
their actual location with

> *. . . in america*
> *ok by me in america*

maria
and the army band
on the west side of wagga

the wind
whisks up a score
as it passes
and tumbles it away

coffees for a road trip

three coffees
on the road today

the first one

> *still asleep*
> *while grinding beans*
>
> *half awake*
> *when the espresso growls*
>
> *the milk is boiled*
> *and ready*

a second cup
two hours away

> *a roaster*
> *turning beans*
> *by the kilo*
> *to brown*
>
> *the smell*
> *caffeine*
> *oil*
> *intensity*
> *pervades the café*

they take their coffee
seriously here

I can't decipher the pattern
a barista has etched
on the frothy top

perhaps a fern
but
I don't know

I drink it down

and a third cup

> *killing time*
> *around a foreign town*
>
> *regular*
> *is super-size*

the cups
and their [lastic lids
are *throw away*
even though
I'm seated right there
at the café table

but the beverage
is warm
and wet

the café filled
with civic officers
on pre-meeting breaks

the chatter
is an undercurrent
a vibrancy
tuned just below the sound
of local radio
which has nothing much
to say to me

for hours

woolshed walk: wattle

not yet
blossom

but soon

woolshed walk: picturing the ethereal

have you got
the i-pad . . .

> *quick*
>
> *set it on*
> *camera*

did we download
the new app . . .

> *go go*
>
> *snap it now*

I want to catch
the sound
of the creek here
rushing
across the rocks

> *now*
> *point it higher*
> *and snap again*

the smell of wattle
is in the air

woolshed walk: the creek

in the foaming rush
the water pools

then
leaps as high
as far
as the air
can carry

    crash

down onto the granite
pool

pool
and fly

woolshed walk: moss march

a tree fell down

lonely for a minute
then . . .

moss march

a rock rolled
then lay still

empty for a minute
then . . .

moss march

the sky was blue
waiting for a sign
when
up the tree. . .

moss march

this
is the time
of the moss march

two voices (tired)

I'm tired enough to want to sleep

    he's tired enough to want some sleep

tired enough to want to keep

    tired enough that he wants to keep

my eyes shut tight all through the night

    his eyes closed

eyes closed tight until the light comes

    his eyes closed

tonight's the night to sleep right through

    tonight's the night if he sleeps right through

tonight I'll sleep the morning too

    he'll sleep into the morning too

I'm tired enough I'll be there till dawn

    he's tired

only open up in the light of dawn

    he's so tired

I'm tired

    sleep

so tired

> *sweet sleep*

I wish tonight be filled to the top

> *fill it up to the brim*

with sleep

> *to sleep*

precious sleep

> *sleep sleep sleep*

I'm tired enough   (*enough*)
I'll close my eyes   (*close your eyes*)
so tired   (*tired tired*)
enough   (*it is enough*)
close my eyes   (*so close your eyes*)
I'll sleep   (*now to sleep*)
only sleep   (*only slee . . .*)

becoming (bella bear)

I once made
a teddy bear

> *cut the fur*
> *against a pattern*
>
> *material tufts*
> *and straying hair*
> *on bulbous shapes*
> *I failed to recognize*
>
> *inside out*
> *and edge*
> *against*
> *another edging*
> *held with little pins*
>
> *inverted*
> *and enjoined*
> *by the detail*
> *of close stitching*
>
> *stray pieces*
> *of random fur*
> *coalesced*
> *reversed*
> *then filled up*
> *to make a body*
>
> *added mouth*
> *a nose*
> *and eyes*
> *a face*
> *new born*

and *bella bear*
became

as though she always
was

free for a little while

and in a little while —
a little while —
the sun
has cleared the edge and fluff
of concealing clouds
that billow
bluff
and blow
around the sky
as though
possessors
license checkers
or taxing agents placing a tariff
on the sunlight
and enforcing rations
for such
is the mentality
of the colour grey
in the season
winter

but
in a little while
just now
in fact
the sun
has found an edge
and light
that casts a golden hue
on green
a glisten
on remnant drops
left behind
by last night's rain
and suddenly the day
is cool spring
and no longer
cold winter

in a little while
just
for a little while
the day
will be made available
to you
and to me
at no cost at all
without restriction
on its purpose

for
a little while

atomic hail and shine

small hail
is leap
and bounding
on the path
that leads to the washing line

leap and bounding
on the grass
that bears its mild beating well

what else
can it do

and as quickly
as this chaos
of bouncing white
(like atoms
in urgent search
of collision)
began
so it ended

and the cloud
that *no further need*
has emptied . . .

moved on . . .

and left the sun behind
to shine

random blows

the rotary-hoist —
sometimes known as
the washing line —
is twirling
in a low blown breeze

the pegs
swaying
to a *clack-clack* tune

the plum tree
a *prunus-see-ya-later-ii*
is waving
as though to say
goodbye

the green plant by
the backdoor
is a constant to-and-fro
that I see as movement
from the corner
of my eye

and I have to look
to check
it is only
a mallow plant

surveying all
and watching me
the magpie
of the oak
who's lookout
is the highest branch

it bends
he sways
as the random breeze
blows

ride day

a saddle
on the sun
and let's go
ride
the sky

black above
and blue below

>
> *yee-ha*
> *yee-ha yee-ha*

bridle
in your hands
stirrup
hold your legs

cowboy
put
your hat on

you better
put your hat on *now*

and ride
we'll ride
right across the sky
ride in a saddle
on a star
we'll ride
our star

>
> *yee-ha*
>
> *yee-ha yee-ha*

climb aboard
low
somewhere near
beginning
of the eastern sky

ride all day
into the west
then

    yee-ha

again

we'll let the sun
go to bed
and keep ourselves
a memory
of the day we rode

    yee-ha
    yee-ha yee-ha

sun lover

sun kisses
through the window
I close my eyes
lover

rivulet
run
down into the hollow
of my throat

sweet kisses from
my lover

and gold

gold shines on the far side
of my eyelids

and gold
colours me
in my skin

sun kisses
through the window

nothing
between me

and
my lover

nova today

the first plum white
is a starburst
nova
on the tree

every branch
is a suspense
of waiting
for the right sun
on
the right day

for the right buzz
of the right bee
nova
waiting

some
can stand no more

no more
no more waiting

and the plum tree
is star bursts

is nova
today

Spring 2017

a bed in passing

sun lies down
on a field of grass

it is not sleeping
just resting

laying its head
on a lover's bed

not sleeping

and this moment too
will pass

axeman: splitting awareness

the splitting axe
is unaware

it rises
and descends

bites and holds
or bounces off

there is only
the wood
only
the reduction
from *that*
down
into *this*

the splitting axe
the swinging blow
is unaware

the axeman
aims his rhythm

it flows like water
in the arc
of *swing* and *strike*

it does not require
thought

and his mind . . .

his mind is in
another place

where the width of the round
upon the block
beneath his axe
is a height
with a bird
at the apex

is a hole in the ground
and a scatter of roots
on their side
standing taller
than he is

is a length
that is a measure
in *board feet*

in *stacked cords*

in *winters warmed*

the swing
of the splitting axe
is unaware

the axeman
is a grunt
an expelled sigh
of air

and silence

shine to sydney

the sun
strikes a jet trail

a gleam in the sky
that is whiter —
brighter —
than the snow

and
another one . . .

streaked across the blue

powering to sydney

while the sun —
so accepting —
makes their journey shine

one silent hour

and now an hour
of silence

no sound

> *the beat of a heart*
>
> *the whisper*
> *of indrawn air*
>
> *the hum of power*
> *through appliances*

the street
seems distant
though it lies
just outside the door

not really very far
at all

and the cars that pass . . .

it is true
that I hear them
but
they are not like
sound
at all

more like my breath
keeping vital functions
alive
and qualified to exist
in the realm
of silence

toast miles at the *brek-café*

I am
the morning crowd
downtown
at the *brek-café*

'cino steaming —
a hiss
a gurgle —
somewhere behind me

strange

I alone
at *brek-café*

you are on the road
I
still here
behind you

you
eating miles

to my
piece of toast
and sunny-side
fried eggs

I will see you
tonight
I will see you
in the morning

fried eggs
long miles

toast for breakfast
alone
in *brek-café*

a bag in a tree (no magpie)

it doesn't seem right
to have a bag
on the tree
in the place
where I'm used to seeing
magpie

a little bit lower
but
that's splitting hairs
on a tree that speaks to me
of morning
and magpie

and it's too high up
to grab it

too high up
to shake it
loose and free

too high
for anything but staring
at a bag
in the tree
where I'm used to seeing
a magpie

it is not right

it is not fair

it is a plastic bag
that holds nothing
but the passing breeze

and a noise
enough
to displace
the magpie

a bomb for jong-un to share with donald

last night I made
a hydrogen bomb
with a small whiff
of sulphide
and a great lack
of aplomb

I used a large cabbage
and a half-dozen eggs
then I threw in a few
of my more sundry
veggie dregs

four big chilis —
because I'm so fire loving —
into a deep casserole
away at the back
of the oven

when I ate it . . .

well well well

I inflated
and then I grew

larger and larger
and quite animated

but it was later
while I was asleep
that I gradually realized
the sulphides
had started to leak

it was too late
to find protection
because that bomb I had made
would not bear
close inspection

and I knew
from the sulphurous smell
that it would explode
and I'd be
going to hell

I should have pleaded

I should have begged

at least I think
I should have cut back
on the eggs

but it was too late
to stop my bomb
so I'll see you in the next life
goodbye goodbye

goodbye
goodbye

goodbye to you all
and so long

rustle russell

russell is
my plastic bag

stuck
up high
in a tree

getting blown around
into scraps of rag

too stuck-up to flee

rustle *russell*
my plastic bag
how can I carry
what belongs to me

when you
my dear
thin
scrap of torn rag
are stuck high
up
in that tree

scaling

> *clugg*
> *clugg*
> *clugg clugg*
> *clugg clugg clugg*

> *clugg*
> *clugg*
> *clugg clugg*
> *clugg clugg clugg*

> *ting*

> *ting*

it's a kind of music

like
a set of scales
played on piano
or ukulele

or
anything really

> *clugg*
> *clugg*
> *clugg clugg*
> *clugg clugg clugg*

that's me
playing a scale
for you

> *clugg*
> *clugg*
> *clugg clugg*
> *clugg clugg clugg*

that's a scale
played for me

    ting

    ting

hip hip
shiraz

a bag of nothing

a plastic bag
held nothing
but wind

now
it holds nothing
at all

for the wind blew
and blew

and the bag

well

you might say the wind
is no substance

you might say the wind
has
no form

but when it blows
like it blew

the bag filled
filled
and tore
until now
it holds nothing
at all

snow blossom

snow caught
on a clear blue day

snow

a flurry
ascending

snow
that sings an air
of spring

blossom
not yet fallen

two fires

I am sitting
in front of my fire
watching a man
in front of his fire
who is somewhere
in africa —
and right there —
on my tv

my flames
are better flames
contained
within a fire box

they warm me
and I can watch —
interested —
the tv

his flames
are better flames
for they are burning
the last wood he has

and his rain
has not yet fallen —
god knows
when it will —
and god knows what will make
his next wood grow

or how
how on earth
he is going to find it

I
am watching
my fire
and I love the flames

I love the heat

and I hope
that man —
my
fire friend —
can find another stick
of wood
to warm him
and cook his food

I hope
he never needs
to feel the cold
rather than the warming
of his fire

battle in the heights

a tug of war

a tugging
of strength

> *who is stronger*
>
> *who will sacrifice
> more*

the tree is tenacious

it will not release
the bag

if the bag
is to free itself
then a twig —
a branch —
will have to be broken

the tree
will not
release

the bag
seems frantic

no price
too high to pay

an accident of fate
and wind
entangled it
and now
the bag seeks nothing more
than release

to fly again

~

in every breeze
the bag flaps
again

seeking freedom

tearing itself
into shreds
but never ceasing

    freedom

if only . . .

if only with the help
of the wind
it could sever a branch . . .

the twig
that holds it

the bag
is in tatters
and ribbons

and as the breeze drops
the bag hangs
limp

it is
exhausted

shopping for breakfast

I ride the magpie

> *my bird*

> *trusty steed*

no need for spur
only me
in the saddle

me
with the bridle
in hand

> *up wings*

> *up wings*

aloft
we rise
and then fly

> *above the neighbouring houses*

> *along the cavernous street*

> *across the paved walk track*
> *and through vacated skate-board park*
> *to land*

the magpie
explorer
is now fossicking
for a garbage bin breakfast

while I —
with a shortlist —
go in
to the shop

to purchase six crumpets
and a carton
of milk

evolving without a picture

I could take a picture
of the transformation
of the tree

the way the bag has ragged
itself

the way nature
acclimatizes
while continuing to change

for in the tree
a bird shape
is perched
up high

on the very
topmost branch

it's so nice to see
a bird shape
where before
was only branches
was only sky

the bird shape
is not frightened
by the rustle
of the bag
with each new passing gust
of wind

the bird shape –
in truth –
does not seem
to mind at all

yet there is something
about the bird shape
that seems
evolved

the shape
that is familiar
is the magpie

but this is not

it has re-formed
into a parrot
re-shaped
into a parrot pair

they bell their sweet calls out
to each other

perhaps
they bell
at plastic bags
as well

I should
have taken a picture
but . . .

it is raining

red aurora

aurora fire-lights

you come to us
even so late
in the season

earthen light
ascending from below
carrying the red
of the heart
the yellow
dancing
towards the sky

and you sound —
you aurora fire-lights —
like thunder

like a terra-train
express running
right through

right through

no stopping

so late this year
yet
here you are
in springtime

aurora

I feel you as a thrash
by jet
of super-heated air

I see you
aurora

dancing lights

the breaking (of roxie's) heart

roxie's on the bark tonight

joe
must have gone out again
and left her

she's going to shout it
all night long

she really misses
her man

~

I live just a little bit
down the road

a road that's
a kind
of canyon

it echoes sound
both
up
and down

and roxie resonates
her

    woo-woo
    woo-wooo-oooo

her

    woo-woo
    woo-woo-oo-oo

she'll resonate
until her joe
comes home

is he out seeing . . .

    woo-woo
    woo-wooo-oooo

    woo-woo
    woo-woo-oo-oo

surely he's not visiting with . . .

    oo-oo-oo-oo

joe is with another

    oo-oo-oo

that *joe*
is with another

    woo-oo woo-oo

she won't stop
until he comes back
home

what can she do . . .

she loves him

what can she do
when
she loves him
so much
that it

    oo-woo-oo

an army of the night

in the night
a black and white army

invisible
against the sky

expert teams

> *holders*
> *cutters*
> *un-wrappers*

worked diligently

and again

they worked
diligently

all through
the long night

it is morning

the tree
is free and clear

> *no sign*
>
> *no sign*

of the invader

> *no sign*
>
> *no*
>
> *no sign*

of the magpie army

yet the bag is gone
as though it never was

and the king sits
on the throne

the magpie throne

once again

axeman: fiddle wish wood

wishbone wood
does not want to be split

axeman
work for your warm

wishbone wood
has got a fiddleback middle
good luck to you
splitting that

axeman
good luck to you

a fork in the wood
is a wishbone growing
like this *and* like
that

growing every way
that is *this* and *that*

axeman
drive your splitter in

axeman
do it again

axeman axeman
drive
drive

drive your splitter
right in

wish bone wood
does not want to be split

it's got a bad case
of fiddleback

hot and strong

these beans
are darker
than the last ones

these beans
are *macho*
in a jar

these beans
are stronger
like a bull stomp

they are
hombres a yay ya

these beans
overpower
when they crush them

these beans
grow stronger
while they wait

these beans
draw a crowd . . .

the people want them

these beans
hat dance
on my hot plate

      a yay yay a
      a yay yay a

these beans
hot dance
on my hat plate

spring in me

I sit outside
I watch

I wait

I let spring
flow in

until the flower
and the bee
are in my veins

I am the grass
I am the tree
I am
the blossom white

I wait —
spring rises —
and I bloom

clouds
fluff around my sky

blue
tempered by a golden sun

the season
buzzes
quietly
as it does its work

spring blooms —
inside me —
and I rise

the sounds of morning

the competing train
of milk
on the stove

the competing train
of espresso

>   *o-o-woa o*
>   *o-o-woa o*

the competing sound
of a storm
on the stove-top

the competing sound
of volcano

>   *f-r-r-a-a-o-o-o-w-w-w*
>   *f-r-r-a-a-r-r-a-a-r-a-o-o-o-w-w-w*

no
no
it is no competition

no
no
no competition
it is only my brew

no competition . . .

that
is just
my coffee

my morning train
of coffee brewed

another (finally)

there has been
another earthquake
my house
is fallen down

the bricks I made
of my sweat
and mud
are mounded
one
upon the other

a monument
of sorts
to what has been
my life

~

there has been another
hurricane
my palm tree
bent itself low
then
was broken

the garden I sang
into green
from the seed
is mud
deeper than
my knees

I am left
with a silted mouth
should I wish
a cup of tea

~

there has been
another flood
this time
in my little room

there
floats my bed

all my possessions
are low
on this river's bed

this time
it was *my* fault

this time *I*
am the one
to blame

for when
I began to weep
I could not stop

the tears I shed
rose and rose
and would not stop

they will not stop —
now —
until I
am finally
drowned

the rotten

here

see

this wood
will be rotten

too easy to heft . . .

too light

there is nothing there

white ants —
their job done —
have moved on

all they have left behind
is some kind
of honeycomb

see how wet
the log is . . .

they prefer the wood
moistened
but
they will eat it dry
just the same

whenever it suits them

and look here . . .

see

this wood
is rotten

you can tell by the white
where the fungus
has been

I have seen it —
sometimes—
grown into mushrooms

still
when it is dry
it will burn
in my fire

don't breathe
the spores

kooka-night goodnight

ack-ack-ack-owoo

kookaburra calls

ack-ack-ack-owoo

the sun
is down below the

ack-ack-ack-owoo

horizon
low
below the world

ack-ack-ack

kookaburra calling
the night to fall

owoo

kookaburra
the last light is gone
the dark is sweeping in

kookaburra will you call

ack-ack-ack-owoo

again

goodnight
kooka-bird

goodnight
my kooka bird

no poet laureates (in a storm)

I wonder what
the poet laureate
would write

what would he or she say . . .

I don't know

no
really
I don't know

> *would they get up on a raft*
> *of kelp and debris*
>
> *would they swim*

no
I do not think
they would

> *would they be*
> *in the rubble*
> *moving rocks this way*
> *moving masonry*
> *out of the road*
>
> *like that*
>
> *just like that*

no
no
I don't think . . .

> *would they hold up a palm tree*
> *bending in half*
> *against the remorseless wind*

no
no
no

what is the good
of a poet
against this wind

> *what is the good*
> *when the water*
> *is rising*
> *over the secret place*
> *where we hid*
> *the gold ducat*
> *that grandmother*
> *treasured*
> *as though*
> *it might have value*
> *beyond the gold*
>
> *she said it would be*
> *mine*
> *one day*

but what would that poet say

> *ay*
> *ay-ay-ay*
>
> *ay-ay-ay-ay*

what is the good of a poet in storm
when my hut is breaking
to pieces
all around me

when my food
is washed out
to the waves
of the sea

when my wife was last seen
holding on to my . . .

    ay
    ay-ay-ay

    ay-ay-ay-ay

I do not think I want
a poet
right now

I do not think I want
a writer

a dreamer

a teller
of tales

no-no-no ay

    ay
    ay-ay-ay

    ay-ay-ay-ay

send food
send materiel

send me water

do not send
a poet

no-no
send us no
poets

    ay
    ay-ay-ay

    ay-ay-ay-ay

I know them
so well

ay yay

I know them
(and their stories)
too well

equinox · xoniuqe

equinox
xoniuqe

it is just as long
and —
either way —
it won't be the same again
until march

long and short
there goes the . . .

equinox
xoniuqe
tonight

just as long
as a daylight hour

equinox

september
spring

an equal day

the wind resolves

the wind has attempted
a resolution
hear the chorale
harmonise
and wail

oh-woo-woo-woo

it will try
to refrain
from song now

ohh-oh-oh

why

said the wind

should I cry so

why
should I moan

no-no-no

I will sing my songs
no more

I will blow
completely in silence

ooh
ooh

only
in silence

ooo-ooo-woo-woo
ooo-ooo-woo-woo

the wind has made
a resolution

hear the chorale wail

   oh-oh-woo

gone (like september)

the plum blossoms

suddenly they are gone
and all I see
is young green

> *where*
> *did white go*

the oaks
are small life
and bud leaves

the view I had
through bare branches
has begun to close

and the cherry flowers
burst —
here and there —
like popcorn

they have outwaited the frost
and now they sing

> *september*
> *is gone*

> *september*
> *is gone*

I don't know
what happened
or when
the change began

but the view from my doorway
is evolving
with every blinking
of my eye

there is a wattlebird
perched
on the magpie throne

there will be trouble on the way
if he stays
but . . .

he has already moved along

nothing is the same

I blame the weather

I accuse
the season

I do not care for changes
that happen every time
I look away

offering day

he stands
under a clear blue sky
sun
directly over head

he holds his offering
high
into the air

a little smoke
rising
then a drifting of blue
away

he offers
to each direction
one to *four*

singing a little offering song
quietly
beneath his breath

shaman
to the spirits
of north and east
west and south

an offering
in the smoke

now
this is *me*

I pour
my roasted beans
from bowl to strainer

chasing
a fluky breeze
that turns me around

Spring 2017

I husk the beans
as I pour them
through the air

a little blue smoke rises . . .

a coffee smell

I offer these
to each direction
as I chase the breeze

a worship sent up
in the smoky air

this is my coffee day

I roast the beans

po-dro – transcribing now

he is under
observation

nothing special about him
just a man
but
under surveillance
from a poetry drone
riding at his shoulder
hanging close

just behind him

watching
what he does

seeing inside
what he thinks

sometimes
framing his thought
a little better
than he could manage
on his own

a little buzz . . .

it is on
the left side

a little buzz . . .

it is on
the right

a hover —
like a question mark —
above him

sometimes

he moves too slow

and sometimes
he thinks *nothing*
about
nothing

nothing at all

the *po-dro* shoots him
with a little
thought-prod

a little
prompt
to action

>   *get on with it*
>   *I have transcribing*
>   *to do*
>
>   *I have transcribing*
>   *of you*
>   *that I have to do*

and so
he pushes on
picks up
a new writing pad

marks it
with a new thought

listens
to the way the wind
comes howling —
comes rattling —
around the windows

and the *po-dro* hums

a little satisfied

self-satisfied

       mmm
       hmmm-hmmm-hmmm

the faint sound
of a stylus etching . . .

a pen
making marks
on paper

the sound of stanza
on top of stanza
in translation from a life
to a
somewhat clever
verse

       mmm
       hmmm-hmmm-hmmm

but
all the time the *po-dro*
is watching
for the next thing
that he does

the next thing
that might be worth
a line or two
of a short poem
about nothing
and a life . . .

a *somehow*
interesting
life

axeman: a way to the wooden heart

he studies the gnarl

a mongreled
angled
fiddled
branch base
with no level surface
to sit on his block
or to face
the splitter

he has
a forty-five degree swing
at best

a recipe
for a broken leg
if he only manages to strike
a glance

the easy thing . . .

the *smart* thing
would be to discard it

there is little usable wood

little
obtainable heat

little *point*
given the mountain of rounds
that remains
to be cut

but . . .

> *what is chopping wood*
> *if it is only slicing*
> *easy*

*what is chopping wood
if you cannot
test yourself
a little*

*an element
of battle*

competition

he looks at his pile
of rounds
selects a fresh one
to serve
as block

sets the mongrel piece
with one angle
jammed
between his chosen block
and another round

kissing the dirt

the other angle—
still jaunty —
is set firm on the block

the striking surface though
has transformed

become horizontal

now
he can study the piece
to see if there is a way
to break its heart

Spring 2017

light now

the evening light
as the sun goes down
turns to blue
outside

the clouds above
are heavy . . .

lending colour
to the scene

and I . . .

I reside inside
in the cosy bright

the lights are on
the fire lit
and suddenly outside . . .

the dark surrounds

but here
is the heart
and here
is the hearth

you and I
are the light now

street sounds (1)

shhh
shhha-shhha-shhherr

shhha-shhha-shhherr shhha-shhha-shhherr
shhha-shhha-shhherr

the wave sound
of a car
raising the tide
of the road
as it boats past outside
upon the street

shhha-shhha-shhherr

the sound moves
rocking both ways

up and down
lap and splash

like living in a grain
of the sand
spread out
to cover a beach

shhha-shhha-shhherr

shhha-shhha-shhherr shhha-shhha-shhherr
shhha-shhha-shhherr

and

sh-sh-sh

barely implied
a long way down the road
but I
magnify
what I hear

    sh-sh-sh

then
suddenly
it is completely quiet

and the only street sound
that remains
is the tinkle
of a twinkling of stars
fallen into water

love (in a time of passing trains)

I have no
ticket

> *just a hiss*
> *then a kiss*

a clatter down the line

doors open
on the platform side

> *in and out*
> *and*
> *in and out*

I wait

> *one north*
> *one south*

go

go

go

go

I don't need
a ticket
to stand
right in the heart . . .

right here
where I am

just a hiss

*just
a kiss*

the door will open
on the platform side

saving daylight

he did best
on part-cloudy days

ragged clouds
that let through
the slanting light
angled down
from the sun

sometimes
he could be seen
in the places
where the rays
came to ground

grabbing
at the air
with his hand

carefully placing
what the hand had caught
inside a fine mesh bag
that showed a rainbow
glistening on its sides
as he moved it

other times
a net . . .

as though chasing
light butterflies

filling up
his fine mesh bags
against a day
of darkness

he knows
a day of darkness
will surely come

he fills up
his fine mesh bags

darkness comes

where you see and feel it

in the stance

in the posture

in a bulging
of the eyes

in the veins

in the breathing

in the rapidness
of the pacing

in the tone

in the volume

in the words
polluting the air

in the clench

in the knuckle

in the sudden disappearance
of distance

in the defiance

in the roar

in the foaming
of the mouth

in the beat

in the rate

in the throat sensation
of a leaping heart

in the exhaustion

in the tremble

in the sense of

oh

oh my god

oh oh

message smoke

corkscrew smoke
rising

a message sent
for me

a billow of cloudy blue
meant for only
my eyes

flakes of ash —
white in grey —
communicate
the wind

blowing my way

the moon has risen early
the sun
is not yet set

fire warms my feet
and the orb
beams down
onto my face

as the twisting flames
sing a song to me
they reach
with their long fingers

and I am mellow now
the smoke has passed
its message gone

whatever it was
I will not know

I am mellow now
and I find
I need not know

four ay-em (the dogs)

the dogs of four ay-em
are yelp
and bark
and whine

they are mayhem

confusion

someone
must have done something
maybe
squeaked a toy

maybe farted

perhaps incontinence
had a role to play

could be
someone slipped in something . . .

spoke a bad word

perhaps there was a robbery
in progress. . .

invitation to a wild response

or those dogs might be
resident inside my head
barking
only inside of me

the dogs of four ay-em
are loud tonight

they speak as one

every one of them
shouting

street sounds (2)

the magpie
heard
all the noise

the lowing cry
of cattle
in the paddock down the road

the sudden application
of air brakes
as the log truck
rounded the corner
too fast
then descended the hill

a dirty drone
of lawn mowers
the bees of *slice*
and *chop*

it heard the hum
of power
rising from the line
beneath its feet

a baby cry

a mobile phone

the magpie heard
all the noise
rising up
from the street below

heard it all . . .

everything

sang a song

a hymn
that rose
above all sounds

rendered them
silent

elementary bachelard

bachelard's words . . .

my imagination

somehow
a story

those old old images
are new

air and water
fire and earth

all material

all
elementary

coffee train

> *too-oot-toot*
> *too-oot-toot*

coffee train
I hear the sound arising

coffee train
beans so brown
surprising

the coffee train
is working up a head of st . . .

> *too-too-oot toot*
> *too-too-oot toot*

the coffee train comes
raising steam
the coffee train comes
raising steam

the coffee train comes

> *toot*

coffee train comes

the coffee train comes
raising s-s-s-s-steam

> *too-oot-toot*
> *too-oot-toot*

> *too-too-oot toot*
> *too-too-oot toot*

coffee train . . .

yes please!

street sounds (3): billows pummelling

the sound pummels
like a billow
from the blue

like a punch
as a car
roars
down the street

> *hear the leaves*
> *feel the buffet*
>
> *the rattle of windows*

a violence blown
in a gasp of power

another car
another gust

another blow

axeman: the man becomes what he always was

it occurs to him

he
is the wood
the wood
of his contemplation

cut now
to suit
this grate
this hearth

burns warm —
mellow —
most of the time

burns hot
the fury of the heart
still
the *rage*

smoulder . . .

no

no need
for smoulder now

he *is* this wood
he knows the way
to cut it
to slice

knows *why* he cuts it
now

contemplates the state
of the diminishing pile
still
some challenge there

Frank Prem

still some knotted gnarls
but
the fiddleback delights him
each time he exposes
a curved wave-pattern

so much to admire
in this
his diminishing pile

he is . . .

    I am

the wood

green no more

introduction to an idea of time

time
is a ritual

>*filled with crumpets*

>*filled with coffee*

it begins
with a book
and a prop against the pillows
in my bed

time
is a passage

>*morning*

>*sun on the glass*

it begins
with a glance
at the green

>*new grown for today*

>*new grown for my eyes*

time
is a ritual

>*look*

>*how the day flies*

sweeping

he held his broom
bristles up
to count them

to check them

to see
that they were
straight and strong

he checked
for pliability

for density

he found them
good

and he began —
as he always began —
in what seemed to him
a corner

a place
that seemed
logical
to begin

there is a rhythm
to sweeping well

a method
to the art

and the sound

    sha

    sha

is regular

is constant
in its depth of sound

and when a man
can find
that perfect pace
he can sweep
right through the hours
of night

and so

he swept
from his beginning place
getting in
behind the dark

and where he swept
you could see
that he had passed that way

for each pull
of the broom
each sweep
in that rhythmic way
brought a little night
with it
left a little
day behind

as he moved along
the sun rolled in
filling every space
he had worked through

he swept
he swept
the whole dark night
away

    so

that's a job well done

so

*that will hold light
for awhile*

so . . .

until another day
has passed

and when the new night
is deep and dark

when it seems
it will never end

he will take his broom
for a bristle count

a straightening check

the density

    sha

and

    sha

    sha

    sha

and

    sha

he will sweep
the daylight back
again

hitch a cloud ride

the sky
is big today

it seems
so endless

I know it is a foolish thing
but
the clouds
seem
up so high

they seem to have come
a long way

they seem to have a long way
still to go

and here am I
just gazing

a pedestrian
beside their road

should I venture
one step . . .

two

should I
put my thumb
in a *hailing* posture . . .

who knows
where a ride
on a cloud
might lead

maybe it just goes
on and on

maybe
it might lead
all the way
to the sun

the sky
is so big
today

I feel so small

I think I will hitch
a cloudy ride
and ask to be dropped off
at the nearest
star

axeman: stacking

even the raggle-taggle
unloading
in the boggy
soggy
wet
of the backyard
last year
was orderly

the first rounds
sank
an inch . . .

more

into the soft

then round
on round
built
in higgledy-piggledy order
up
and out

until
there was a mountain
of unsplit rounds
packaged up

now
this job
is about un-packing

round after round
down
onto firm ground

to chop
to dry off

a new mound —
after the splitter —
of cut wood

cordwood

until it is too high

too near
to the block

until
he cannot cut more

then —
with reluctance —
he focuses
on stacking

into the corral
built from freight crating

a floor
to keep the cut wood
off the ground

sides
to keep the stack upright

to provide
firm boundaries

barrow after barrow

> *from the surrounds*
> *of the chopping block*
>
> *a few short paces*
> *to the corral*
>
> *then stack*

straight lines
angled backwards
so that any slippage
will be *into* the frame

this
is the less enjoyable task
but
it must be done

straight
dry
stacked rows

and then . . .

back
to the block

cut some more

the wind and the lion

I call on the lion

    let him roar

    let him roar

I call on the lion

    let him roar

king? let him rule

in the jungle and
the savannah too

I call on the lion

    let him roar

I blow through his mane

    hear him roar

whisper his name

    hear him roar

friend? I am no fool

the jungle
let him rule

but
I know the lion's name

    let him roar

axeman: shared energy

weary

he began

>   *position the round*
>
>   *swing*
>
>   *strike*

again

>   *position the round*
>
>   *swing*
>
>   *strike*

there is an invigoration
an energy
that communicates itself to him
in reverse

from the struck wood
into the blade –
back upward –
through the handle
into him

instead of compounding
his weariness
retreats

when the first round
is split
he automatically
selects another

position the round

swing

strike

his vigour —
now located —
does not flag
through an hour
of repetitions

position the round

swing

strike

and he feels
deeply pleased
at what he has accomplished
after such an
unpromising
beginning

sough intent

the roar of the wind —
like the pounding
of surf —

is breaking
constantly

this night
it is rain
that gives the wind
body

a presence as physical
as it is
implied

my lamp dims
to the sough
of deeper seas

blown
and blown

intense
is the night

a little behind

I am a little way
behind the wind

>*if I do not push
>how will it blow*

mine is the space
where energy
amassed
awaits release

>*which way
>should the breeze*

~

I am a little behind
the sea

>*if I do not swim
>how can
>the tide*

mine is the space
for sidelong strokes
and building waves

>*rocking waters
>to and fro*

~

I am
some distance
behind the sun

if I
do not burn
how long
the night

if I find
I cannot burn . . .

how long
how dark
will the night

on a scale (of tree)

on a scale of
you
to *me*

I am down below

you are lost
in air
up there

yours is a scale
of *further yet*
to go

while I am down here
waiting

~

on the scale
of *me*
to *you*

you diminish
in the distance

fall away
or
fly away

while I *am*

yes
I *am*

down below

she walks (the shapely eucalypt)

she walks

>*a sway built
into her gait*

she walks

>*moving like
she knows the way*

she walks

>*I stand
and watch her passing*

I stand

>*she walks
the day stills*

for a moment of time
hold fast

while
she walks
a-
way

poemminer

I have been mining now
for half my life

maybe more

digging
and
always digging
deeper

I excavate
a black seam
in the hope —
the yearning hope —
that
what I find
will be gold

the deeper I push
with my shovel
and pick

with my hands

the blacker
the darker
the more golden
my findings

I do not believe
I could —
now —
find a way
to stop

the black gold
has claimed me
for the days . . .

for the *rest* of the days
of my life

but
that
is no hardship
to me
with my tools in my hand

I am a miner

the deeper I go
the clearer the darkness
until even the mysteries . . .

until
I understand them

I shine my light
in
illumination

I have been mining
a black seam
a dark seam
for thirty long years

maybe more

every time
I strike
with my pick into the black
I feel hope
anew

a solemn hope —
renewed —
that I might find . . .

will find
gold

axeman: towards completion

contemplation
becomes a form of pleasure

glancing from the house —
from his breakfast —
to the diminished woodpile
he is able
to visualise

>	*less*

>	*less*

>	*none*

>	*nothing*

there are only a few steps
now
that remain
between

>	*work to be completed*

and

>	*job done*

as he looks out
to the solid rounds
that remain

he can contemplate
a completion

the lizard saurs

the lizards are out

the first skinks
of spring
are exploring the covered patio

> *circling*
>
> *discovering the dimensions*
>
> *becoming aware of*
> *surfaces*
>
> *boundaries*
>
> *obstacles*
>
> *each other*

they come forward
at a rapid clip
to meet

snout
to
snout

then a flick

a twist

one is off
run-slithering away

sliding
around a corner

airborne
in his haste

the other
perhaps a millimetre larger
in length
or girth

or attitude

is in pursuit
and he will not stop

he will not stop

he skids around a corner

he will not stop

until he *alone*
has possession
of the patio

axeman: await winter

I am the wood
and I am
the axe

I am the man
charged
with cutting through
a mountain

and I hew

and I chop

I reduce the round
by slice and by chip
and by break
through the *rough*
opened up in the grain

I touch the bark
run my hand over the splinters
I have raised
through the raining down
of my blows

and I find I am moved
by the feel
of *rough*

by the colours
I have exposed

almost sorrow . . .

almost
I sorrow

but . . .

another round goes up
on the splitting block
and I swing
in the act of striking new blows
to reduce the thing
to a smaller thing

to make me warm
once
before burning

then I lay them down —
in a last act —
sedate in rows
that wait on the winter

as I —
sedate now too —
await winter

the noise of writing

my neighbour has got the

    doof doof doof

I think he picked it up
from the radio

I am sitting here
and making big noise

my pen is

    scratch-scratch-scree

all over the paper
hear me roar

all over the paper

my neighbour has got the

    brr-umm-rrumm-rrumm

I think he picked it up
with some car keys

I'm here revving my engines
loud

    scrr-scrr-scrr scrr-scrr-scrr

turning over my pen
onto the paper

I'm turning over
a pen
on the paper

hear me start

my engine
roar

street sounds (4): rain care

a car washes
up the road

      ssshhhhwwooowwwrrrraaaarrrhhh

as the rain

      tappa-tappa-tappa-tap

      ta-ta   *ta-ta*

comes down

the street runs
like a river flows

the cars drift by
like powered boats

and the rain cares less
than naught

      tappa-ta   *tappa-ta*

bouncing
spreading wide
upon the tin
the rain cares
nothing

      ssshhhhwwooowwwrrrraaaarrrhhh

cloud like

the mystery of clouds
is . . .

well
I don't really know

they just billow
before my eyes

like living a storm

thunder
rang the night
last night

thunder
brought the rain

I know that the cloud
that brought it
has gone now

away
like mist on the breeze

like a thought
now distant
but I wonder . . .

was it a cloud
like *you*

just
like you

bass lines

    doo-do-do-do doo-doo-doo-d

    doo-do-do-do doo-doo-doo-d

    doo-do-do-do doo-doo-doo-d

the bass line
is an insinuation
by the café stereo system

playing noise
pitched just above
the sound of

    clatter-clatter-cla-cla-cla-cl

    clatter-clatter-cla-cla-cla-cl

and

    shu-shu-shu-shu   shu shu sh sh

    shu-shu-shu-shu   shu shu sh sh

voices interspersed
tell the state of things

the bread
just out of the oven

    doo-doo-doo-do

another flat white
wanted now

takeaway

    shu-shu-shu   sh

clean up
after table five please

    clatter-clatter-clatter-cl

    clatter-clatter-clatter-cl

the bass line
on the café stereo system is

    doo-do-do-do   doo-doo-doo-d

    doo-do-do-do   doo-doo-doo-d

an insinuation

elm husks fleeing

the husks of spring
are fleeing
staying *just ahead*
as the wind blows

they are trying madly
to evade it

to crash-land
in a heap
of their fellow hop-husks

in small seas
that ripple
beneath
the blown breath

of storm-before-summer
of thunder-in-a-blast-of-hail
of turbulent-black-that-falls-
in-the-middle-of-the-day

in the middle of the day
husks flee the wind

cuckoo you

the bed was laid
with good intent

> *old rot*
> *new dirt*

a garden mountain
for me to dig
and water
and
for planting

alas
the time that passed

alas
the things that seemed
more important

never mind
never mind
here we are
right now

> *get the shovel*
> *turn it over*

> *start anew*
> *in that good dirt*

> *kikuyu grass*
> *hardy soul*
> *tenacious grasp*

> *a spreader*

> *an invader*

> *a controller*

Spring 2017

alas
the time that passed

    cuckoo

alas
the things that seemed . . .

    cuckoo

    cuckoo

    cuckoo

first clouds of november

goodbye

going places

farewell

you leave

I
on my back —
aground —
just watching

for someone . . .

always
someone
must remain behind

goodbye

I see you leaving

goodbye
goodbye

~

don't deny
your unravelling

I see you in the sky

like a drop of white
into the blue

I see you ravelling . . .

unravelling

drifting through
the colour
that holds you

    blue

    blue

and you

~

angel kiss

I think
you are blushing

I think
I'm sure
you are blushing

have you been kissed before . . .

no

no
you are too naïve

too insecure

but
oh
you are lovely

how lovely you are

angels kiss

they know the ones

they kiss
only the right ones

are you blushing

~

somebody dabbing
abstract clouds

somebody got
the paintbrush out

    dab

    dab

abstract
here and there

and there

abstract brush

somebody got
an abstract brush

    dab

    dab

we'll call it
cloud

    dab dab

we'll call it a cloud

abstract

somebody
with an abstract brush

call it a cloud

the bazaar

> *misterr misterr*

> *I got a day for you*

> *what sorrt a day*
> *you want*

> *misterr*

> *misterr*

he walked
slowly
but determinedly
through the bazaar

taking in the sounds

> *misterr misterr*

and the sights

letting the whole
hyperactive
milieu
with its raucous cacophony
wash over him
as he walked

> *I got a day*

> *what sorrt a day*
> *you want*

> *I got sun*
> *got moon*

> *got storrm and rrain*

> *misterr*

Frank Prem

you want day verry clear
I got

hey
misterr

today
was for strolling

for atmosphere
and familiarity

tomorrow
he might bargain
a little

bicker

to acquire
his weather

axeman: good for another

he leans against a post
at the corner of the stack
while he takes a blow

the sweat runs easy
and his breath comes hard
he has been swinging
to a rhythm

and round after round
has fallen at his feet
new opened
with the wood
glowing pink
and the pile he has cut
getting bigger

and the pile
beside him —
of the rounds still to cut —
showing smaller

he re-lives
as he catches
at his straining breath

> *every blow*
> *that flew sideways*
> *from a narrow grab of wood*
>
> *every blow*
> *that stuck fast*
> *because he caught the round*
> *too near the centre*

too much
or too little
he is bashing his way
from outside to in

and —
as his breath
grows easy —
he knows he is good
to go another round

and another round

stalk? heron!

I stalk the heron

the heron
does not know

does not care

she has a needle beak

a zorro mask

long legs

the heron
has long legs

the heron has my
back yard

I stalk the heron

with an i-pad

[snap]

.
.
.

[snap]

.
.
.

gotcha

yeah

the dismissal of the doona

I told it

> *you*
> *I shall not want*
> *again*
> *until morning*

and flung

a bird
a bat
the pterodactyl
beneath which I
had been sleeping

it took a draggled leap

a tangle
rising
up
up

then
beneath the weight
of its own cottoned wings
it fell —
dead —
beside me

> *so be it*

I said aloud

> *in the morning*
> *when the cool descends*
>
> *then*

Spring 2017

*you and I
will continue this discussion
from positions that hold
mutual warmth*

of the sun

I will hide myself
inside a cloud today

I have no need
of the sun

I have no need
of the light

no need for blue

the day is grey
no matter what

I will hide myself
as mist
with all
the other mist

inside a cloud

I have no need

no other need

Spring 2017

the old man's stock take

he called it
taking stock

>sitting
>in the sun
>
>in the shade
>
>beneath the veranda awning
>when it rained
>
>considering the garden
>and the green grass
>
>counting the bees
>
>white butterflies
>
>bugs rising
>on transparent wings
>with the sun
>shining through
>
>a tiny halo of light
>around each
>
>the wind at play
>through washing
>hung to dry
>
>and of course
>the swaying
>of his trees
>
>his beloved trees
>in full summer leaf
>with a rich depth
>of green
>to show

taking stock
he called it

to me
it appeared
he was sleeping

forgotten: the night

I was the forgotten one

the day
the sun forgot

left churning
in the dark

no ray of light
no beaming smile
ever found me

the chill
of colour *sable*
I made my own

turned my back
on belated entreaties
turned my back
to *sorry* sounds

turned my back
on day

I claim
the night

I *am* the night

Frank Prem

a gleam in shadow

there is no shine
like the shine that glints

a knife
below the moon

a star
hidden
within a shadow

do not approach
the stellar shine
that knifes
beneath the moon

the shadow waits

the shadow
in
the shadow

supposed: music

> *rrrreeeeee*
> *pa-dee-pa-da-da (oh yeh)*
>
> *ree-pa-dee-pa-da-da (yeh yeh)*
>
> *peep-eep-eep-a-da-da (yeh-eh)*

music
he supposed

jazz . . .

perhaps

he isn't sure

> *pa-da-da (yeh yeh)*

it's just there
in his head

sounding like
a trumpet

a sax

something brass

> *rrrreeee-pa-da*
>
> *da da*
>
> *pa da-da-da*
>
> *rrrreee-ee (yeh yeh-yeh-yeh)*

some piano
too
all the time

he wishes

sometimes
he wishes

    pa-da-da

that it would just
stop

    (*yeh*)

down the rain

the rain is falling
arrow straight

striking birds
still on the wing

they struggle
in their wish
to fly

an arc described
with raindrops shattering
at each attempt
by wings
to drive

where do they fly
where do they
need
to go
on such a day
of pouring down

the answers
are fleet
feathers flying

on the wing

and still the rain falls
striking

straight down

a sea above

it sounds
like a wave

the roof
is serving as a beach
of sorts

tin sheeting
the equivalent
of sand

the wind
makes the tide rise
softly moaning
makes the tide
ebb away

makes a sigh
of flotsam on the move

and the clouds
are a drifting sea

there is
no end to them
and I think . . .

there is
no end to them
and I feel . . .

the ocean
that is above me
is going to rain

is going to rain
forever

breath

and I wonder
how long
I can hold my breath

there is danger
in the air
all around me

decisions —
dark decisions —
are pending
and I don't know . . .

I
just don't know . . .

so I am holding
my breath
until
it is safe again

and I wonder *how long*
until it is safe
again

I wonder how long
until I can breathe

no sheriff day

I could not call
the sheriff

he would not come
there is no crime

more
it is just a feeling
of *something wrong*

sometimes
a threat to me

sometimes
an outrage

sometimes
as though it is my own fault

as though it is me

in any case
I am on my own

me
and my dangers

me
and my fears

me
and the problems
I cannot comprehend

cannot
resolve

long day . . .

it is such a long
long day

perhaps
I should abandon it

maybe I
should stay
beneath the blankets
in my bed

under the sun (in the backyard)

there is water
on the grass

that is dew
I suppose

waiting for the day
to bear down
and burn it away

meanwhile

meanwhile

the bees are amok
among
the clover flowers

a fat old wasp
is hovering
around the back door
maybe thinking about
a new nest

    not there
    my dear
    not there

away she goes
as though my thought reached out
and . . .

large white
and small grey butterflies
have been warmed up
among the grasses

the cabbages

Spring 2017

a lizard
saunters
in promenade
across the doorstep

a little *saur*
a very long
long tail

a proud skink
under
a warm balm

the day
is ruffling a self-sewn
peach tree

such a tender green

so . . .

so very
optimistic

the oak trees too
feel the need to wave
their new summer growth

under the backyard sun

dark song

the moon above me
sings
her song

cold gold
the dark away

I alone
in colours

pearl
and chequer shades

I hear her singing

I hear her song

she needs no voice
to be the harmony
of silence

and so
the song is sung
for me
alone

cold gold
and the dark
away

fading

and what
when I can no longer see
the dappled light

>*the green*
>*the gold*
>*the blue*

playing to me
through the half opened blind
hanging across my window

what then when *black*
replaces the butterflies
dancing among the herbs
and flowers there

is there still to be
a butterfly shape
but coloured in the hue
of *night*

I can see
the gentle movement
wind
shivering the stems

and sunlight dazzling
a colour not green
not gold
but *glory*

what
when day fades
even before
night has come

what will I gaze on then

the shop

christmas cakes
red wrapping

green

santa
and rudolph
shaped from hammered tin
and a coat of paint

no room in the sleigh
after the christmas crackers
and bon bons

and baubles

fairy lights
wait for the dark
to come

silky

the silky oak
my honey trap

I am caught

held

sweet tendril fingers

for the drinking

once a year
the honey comes

running
sweet
like water

gold
is not a hue
to do it justice

the silky oak —
today —
is more colour
than the sun

and the honey
is there —
right there —
for the drinking

bloom burst

the stamens
have begun
rising

the allium
is bursting
to bloom

fish (clouds)

my fish swims
a sea of blue

my fish
hunts
in the deep

and in shallow

~

my fish
swims
among the clouds

leaping

through the blue

ahead of
thunder

cry cloud

hidden
inside a curl
of cloud

a little weeping

a little rain

whistling

here am I
whistling the wind

waiting
for my storm
to sing

and to roar

mining the farm (for bottled water)

I am a miner —
it is true —
but
I am also
a farmer

whereever I buy
I work the land

grain
in grain country
apples
in the hills

I could argue
that I farm my places
better
than they have ever
been farmed before

> *look at the yield*
> *from the wheat last year*
>
> *look*
> *at the condition I've got*
> *on every lamb*
>
> *the apples*
> *would green*
> *my old granny*
>
> *and the pears*
> *are a beauty*
> *to behold*

so don't try to tell me
I am no farmer

I grow weary
of hearing
that kind of thoughtless thing

and it is true
that I am also mining
water
but
there is plenty here
right here
in the ground

and it is *me*
now
who owns this land

and I will mine
what is mine
and I will farm it

and the rest of you

all
of the rest of you
can go to hell
and just be damned

silent we

I watch
in silence

you watch
in silence

between us
we say
nothing

~

somewhere
something happened

somewhere . . .

again

I say

you say

nothing

allium bee

allium bee

allium bee

bee beware
the flavour
on your breath

~

an onion acreage

a bee
to roam

much
to do

and all alone

in the path

we
who stand
in the path of the storm

may flare
our lightning

roar thunder

breaking

breaking bread

the *ritual*
of breaking bread

he wonders
as he glances along the table

> *relatives*
> *dear ones*
>
> *not so dear*
>
> *no*
> *some not so dear*
> *at all*
>
> *talk and talk and eat*
> *and*
> *pass the salt along*
>
> *the wine*
>
> *ha ha*
>
> *a merry jest*
>
> *ha ha*
> *so*
> *humorous*

everyone
at table
and all of them
breaking bread

he wonders
will he see them
again

he wonders
does he hope to

he has nothing
in common
with these breakers of bread
except . . .

the ritual

the occasion

the
affirmation

of breaking bread

just once a year
he breaks his bread
and glances
along the table

wonders
if he still belongs
here
with these

to break this bread

waltz mote

I watched
for a time

I had to choose
among the colours

among the drifters

discern
amongst the rhythms
that moved them

the lights
that illuminated them

I had to choose one
that was pretty

and then
I joined in

we moved around

we shone
and we sparkled
around
and around

we danced

around and around
and
around and around

the last remaining
on the dance floor

one more twirl around
in the light

then we parted
and the music . . .

nocturne

it spreads
like a sigh
out of the silence
of the night

only a dog

    yipping

    yapping

only the shadows
stirring

and the murmur
rolling down
from the height
of the hill

the car
ploughing darkness
is a ghost
of after-light
herding the wind
before it

chauffeuring this
nocturne
somewhere deeper

clear the way

pencils

water colour pencils

these
the best
that he has

> a rainbow
> of colours
>
> charcoals
>
> and graphite

pristine paper
a brush

some water

contemplating his task
he had concluded
that nothing but the best
of his tools
would be adequate
today

he lightly sketched

> his mother
>
> his father
>
> his brothers
> and sisters
>
> their wives
> and husbands
>
> their children

his children

uncles

aunts

he drew them all
lightly
in good likeness
with his charcoal

filled the paper

populated it

lastly
he drew himself
in the top corner
looking down

he drew his love
in the bottom corner
looking up at him
across the crowded scape

choosing colours
carefully
he began the next work
quickly shading in
a garden

flowers

dragonflies

magpies and parrots

shrubs
and trees

divided by the shape
of a winding path
that ran from the top corner
to the bottom

brush wetted
he worked water
into the areas
of his garden

washing in
the colours
and shapes

when he was done
his garden
was in bloom

his trees in full leaf

the birds
alive
in their colours
and shades

and the path
winding
yet direct
from the top corner
to the bottom corner

the way
completely clear

After Words

Author Information

Frank Prem has been a storytelling poet since his teenage years. He has been a psychiatric nurse through all of his professional career, which now exceeds forty years.

He has been published in magazines, online zines, and anthologies in Australia, and in a number of other countries, and has both performed and recorded his work as spoken word.

Frank is an Adjunct Research Associate of the School of Education, Charles Sturt University, Australia.

He lives with his wife in the beautiful township of Beechworth in North East Victoria, Australia.

Connect with Frank

Find Frank at his website www.FrankPrem.com, or through Social Media online at Facebook, X (Twitter), Instagram and YouTube.

Other Published Works

Archive

A Poetry Archive – Volume 1 (2024)
A Poetry Archive – Volume 2 (2024)
A Poetry Archive – Volume 3 (2024)
A Poetry Archive – Volume 4 (2024)
A Poetry Archive – Volume 5 (2025)
A Poetry Archive – Volume 6 (2025)
A Poetry Archive – Volume 7 (2025)

Memoir

Small Town Kid (2018)
The New Asylum (2019)

Picture Poetry Series

Pilgrim Volume 1 - Illustrated by Leanne Murphy (2024)
A Lake Sambell Walk (2021)
A Few Places Near Home (2023)

Children's Picture Books

The Beechworth Bakery Bears (2021)
Waiting for Frank-Bear (2021)
On Allium Avenue (2025)

Bachelard Interpreted

A Choir of Whispers (2024).
A Cleansing Flame (2024)
Real Weight (2025)
A Flight Of Ideas (2025)
An Ocean of Purity (2025)
The Kiss Reverberant (2025)

Speculative Poetry

The Garden Black (2022)
A Specialist At The Recycled Heart (2022)
The Cielonaut (2024)

A Love Poetry Trilogy

Walk Away Silver Heart (2020)
A Kiss for the Worthy (2020)
Rescue and Redemption (2020)
Alive Is What You Feel (2023)

Natural Disasters

Devil In The Wind (2019)
Of Drought and Fire (2025)
SMALL Change (2025)

War and Conflict

Sheep On The Somme (2021)
From Volyn To Kherson (2023)

Free Verse

Pebbles to Poems (2020)
White Whale (2024)
Ida: Searching for The Jazz Baby (2023)
Herja, Devastation With Cage Dunn (2019)

What Readers Say

Small Town Kid

A modern-day minstrel. Highly recommended.
  —A. F. (Australia)

Small Town Kid is a wonderful collection.
  —S. T. (Australia)

Devil In The Wind

Trust me, this book will stay with you. Bravo!
  —K. K. (USA)

Moving, beautiful, and terrible. I was left with a profound sense of respect, as well as a reminder that we should never take for granted every precious every moment of life.
  —J. S. (South Africa)

The New Asylum

Words can't do justice to the emotional journey I travelled in (reading this collection).
  —C. D. (Australia)

If I had to pick one book over the past year that has truly resonated with me, this would be it.
  —K. B. (USA)

Walk Away Silver Heart

Instantly grips you by the throat in his step-by-step story of survival. Bravo!
  —K. K. (USA)

Outstanding!
  —B. T. (Australia)

A Kiss For The Worthy

A Celebration of Life Written in Thoughtful Bursts of Poetic Expression
—C M C (United States)

With every verse, I found myself reflecting about myself, my life, and the world.
—K

Rescue and Redemption

The passion of love in its many forms explored by one for another.
—J L (United States)

I've enjoyed every word, every breath. Every moment within the life of these stories.
—C D (Australia)

Sheep On The Somme

Museums and archivists take note--sell this in your gift shops, preserve it in your archives. Professors, teachers--share with your students.
—A R C (United States)

(This) book is a beautiful and graphic tribute to all those brave men and women who gave their lives for their countries between 1914 and 1918.
—R C (South Africa)

Ida: Searching for The Jazz Baby

I found myself deeply moved by the presentation of Ida's elusive, illusionary life.
—E G (United States)

He gives her a depth and vulnerability that the press didn't.
— A C (United Kingdom

The Garden Black

Prem creates verse that illuminates our world, its experiences and history.
—S C (United Kingdom)

Prem's poetry reminds that life is fragile and fleeting ... both harsh and beautiful.
—D G K (Canada)

A Few Places Near Home

The author has captured many beautiful images in this book, and is a wonderful photographer as well as a poet. This book would make a beautiful coffee table book filled with moving prose to make us ponder with gorgeous accompanying images.
—D K (Canada)

Index of Poems

A

a bag in a tree (no magpie) 513
a bag of nothing 519
a bed in passing 507
a bomb for jong-un to share with donald 514
absent friends (snap) 172
a casual meeting with the banjo 128
a coffee break 293
a coffee song 87
a fisher of storms 168
after storm 16
a gleam in shadow 624
a good girl 81
a good season (down at the creek) 36
a husqy roar 67
air china 242
a jonquil song 481
a journey of raindrops 15
a line of brothers 339
a little behind 590
a little light (darker) 68
a little privacy please 469
allium bee 646
alone (with the wind) 93
a long wave 282
an accusation boogie 180
an alchemy 21
an army of the night 532
anonsom bul 24
another (finally) 538
a pattern 380
artist enough 182
art to be light (by and by) 478
a sea above 628
asparagus spring 480
at brunetti's 430
atomic hail and shine 498
a towel to ride 241

a trio of contemplations 348
at the social security office 268
a wake in lockington 96
a waking wind 429
a west side story – wagga in the park 485
a-wooing for coffee 218
axeman: a philosophy of the woodpile 216
axeman: await winter 599
axeman: a way to the wooden heart 557
axeman: axe bound 116
axeman: axe time 466
axeman: fiddle wish wood 534
axeman: good for another 615
axeman: oh fiddleback 84
axeman: shared energy 587
axeman: splitting awareness 508
axeman: stacking 583
axeman: the man becomes what he always was 575
axeman: towards completion 596

B

bakery sparrow 77
bass lines 605
battle in the heights 523
bear in 261
becoming (bella bear) 495
before her majesty 205
belle and beau 53
beneath the oak 174
benedicted by the day 251
best words (repainted) 46
bird on the menu 97
birthday surprise (an occasion unravelling) 100
bloom burst 639
bones (just bones) 112
bowing before (my) royalty 20
breakfast 474
breaking 648
breath 629

C

can't trust the rice 188
cherishing 351
chopping a cord 144
chortle magpie 482
claiming credit 98
clear the way 652
climbers rescued 124
climbing 146
closing time 400
cloud like 604
coffee café before late shift 31
coffees for a road trip 487
coffee train 573
collage (ti-ri-ol) 447
concerto 341
conditional garden 114
coyote moon 12
creative space 356
crescent tonight 367
cry cloud 641
cuckoo you 608
currawong cries 426

D

daily: the splits 45
dancing the fire in the evening 10
dark song 634
dark substance 358
deep breathing 384
digestive fibonacci: fractal-izing mandelbrot 17
dissatisfiction 91
don't mind the toll 271
down the rain 627
down without care 11
dragonfly summer 275
dream hunt 316

E

elementary bachelard 572
elements of the tapestry 201
elm husks fleeing 607

empty starlings 454
equinox - xoniuqe 547
eucalyptus farewell 236
evolving without a picture 527
except the fire 5

F

fading 635
faux song in the city 439
fending 437
finding north 39
finding the colour 319
first clouds of november 610
fish (clouds) 640
five bird poems (benalla) 423
floe 225
fly 378
fly high prayer 382
for a magpie 72
forgotten: the night 623
for me 368
for the drinking 638
for your (brunetti) birthday 431
four ay-em (the dogs) 569
free for a little while 496
friend (no friend) at the door 374

G

gaston, my canard, teaches fantasy 176
getting lucky 312
go and pick (ordering alliums) 402
goat dance #1 308
go gather berries 336
gone (like september) 550
goodnight colours 295
goodnight, my western sky 19
green lady 187
groucho spy-pies 464

H

hammer love 107

harmony (minor) 459
heaven glimpsed (leaves down) 383
he dreams while the corvids dance 296
here 61
hitch a cloud ride 581
hoary hoary 405
honking to be one 162
hot and strong 535
hot one 209
how it begins 445
how rain starts 42
how (to hell) 230
hume dam – away to freedom 6
humming 372

I

ibis to land 449
imagination (patter pitter) 70
in jerusalem 366
in pursuit 298
inside 355
inspired to leave 265
interpreting signals 193
in the cloud 235
in the day 376
in the path 647
in the room 272
into sleep 337
introduction to an idea of time 577
I on solid ground 178
is creating the divine 8
I think a feeling (in words) 33
it waits for me 29

J

job of the day 127
just chili (not dangerous) 373

K

kooka-night goodnight 542

L

last 228
last one 139
last remains 408
lazy moon 30
learning to read by inches 160
let the runners run 211
light now 559
like rain 279
like summer (to me) 143
line dancers 254
looking up 22
lotus emergent 43
love (in a time of passing trains) 562
low hanging 56

M

making home 273
march is here 289
marliess-opolis 317
message smoke 568
might as well 401
mining the farm (for bottled water) 643
mock orange 240
museum #1 – the museum jungle 434
museum #2 – in the trenches 435
museum #3 – the whale 436
my a*** belongs to the government 131
my love tonight 252

N

new coffee 443
news 246
nocturne 651
no poet laureates (in a storm) 543
no sheriff day 630
not (at all) 103
not today 255
nova today 503

O

offering day 552
of the second breeze 333
of the sun 620
old birds refrained 150
on a scale (of tree) 592
once a hole 411
one form of 'good morning' 331
one silent hour 511
one step new place 334
on peaceful streets 223
on the green 325
on the wind 60
oonga boonga (power to the people) 415
orchestrated autumn 328

P

persepctive 243
picking wild sunshine 213
ping pong, under certain conditions 184
po-dro – transcribing now 554
poemminer 594
power lines 259
power talk 258
prepare your home 276
pretty day 352
prowling in black and white 462
puppet show: the foyer 433

Q

quality light 55

R

random blows 499
random city 432
raven 521
ready for a feed (baby magpie) 73
red aurora 529
red (betelgeuse) 281
reducing the rounds 75
reek assessment 207
renewable 335

resident wind 249
returnee (the heroine of there and back) 238
ride day 500
ride the portent 89
rising above ground 57
river call to morning 13
rough love 120
ruffling the skin 170
rustle russell 516

S

saving daylight 564
scaling 517
scent of ambrosia 219
sea bed 302
seasonal 154
season to season 389
sea, the desert 278
secrets of the sough 95
seeing through 345
sentinel 477
shadow march 475
she walks (the shapely eucalypt) 593
shine to sydney 510
shoe dance 41
shopping 198
shopping for breakfast 525
shush-ing the oak tree 404
silent we 645
silky 637
size and stature 263
slaking the forest 327
sleepy 377
slippage 301
snow blossom 520
sog descending 450
so handsome (what a guy) 364
somewhere else 118
song rules today 248
sough intent 589
sound returns 227

speaking of this and that (after the fall) 342
spring creek radio 35
spring in me 536
stalk? heron! 617
stars in his sleeves 27
stealing the soul (just a little bit) 62
still (day) life 428
stilling wrath on the horizon 105
storm free 170
strange times 472
street echo 468
street sounds (1) 560
street sounds (2) 570
street sounds (3): billows pummelling 574
street sounds (4): rain care 603
stripping 409
sulphur-crested christmas fools 175
sun lover 502
supposed: music 625
sweeping 578
sweet blow-in 257
sweet old song 473

T

tarn-tarn OOF! – a rain dance 122
tenderfoot dancer 79
the air-craft of kitchen utensils 452
the bazaar 613
the beginning of life 37
the breaking (of roxie's) heart 530
the crocodile trainer 136
the day away 222
the dismissal of the doona 618
the drafter 362
the eye 314
the gentle art 290
the green and the brown 253
the hunt for the wild arancini 456
the last annual show 134
the last red delights 152
the lizard saurs 597

the magpie song 444
the name on the grave 'who am I' 460
the nascent days of vicugna air 306
the noise of writing 601
the old man's pigeons 58
the old man's stock take 621
the old pen 108
the pictured book 244
there - at the gorge 9
the rotten 540
the school cleaner 418
the shop 636
the slap 321
the sounds of morning 537
the thought, write? 477
the wet september why 28
the wind and the lion 586
the wind at war 90
the wind resolves 548
three birds: pigeon, magpie, rosella 7
three faces in a car 370
three presentations 48
thwock-ing turbulence 220
tidying up the kitchen migraine 109
time awareness 203
time is up 388
toast miles at the brek-café 512
today the time 34
too cool for (magpie) school 65
torrent and warm 25
towards a naming 303
trade-ie wars/replacing a water heater 165
transcribing from the original 214
tree poem 63
trench man #1: the trench man's tools 390
trench man #2: almost (so far to go) 391
trench man #3: to the end or until 393
trench man #4: home before texture 394
trench man #5: the nature of the job 395
trench man #6: foreign substance 396
trench man #7: staggered end 397
trench man #8: to achieve the cool 398

tweedling october 51
twice packing the pigeons 195
two fires 521
two totters 191
two voices (tired) 493

U

under the sun (in the backyard) 632
unravelling the code 329

V

veil dance (oh no) 440
venus of the eucalypts 138
vetting for the ramen restaurant 244
victorian war memorial 070717 438
victory (over hornets) 353
voices know (wo-wo-wo) 233

W

waiting westerly 359
waltz mote 650
wattlebird sprinkle 117
wearing down 226
weather 470
weather forecasting 158
weather war 323
what day is this 360
what did you do today 284
what is, if it won't 361
where you see and feel it 566
whistle if 406
whistling 642
who will leave you clean 26
willing the oak 347
wind-jig day 310
winter oh 387
wired awake 483
with ghosts 126
Woolshed in Spring 44
woolshed walk: moss march 492
woolshed walk: picturing the ethereal 490

woolshed walk: the creek 491
woolshed walk: wattle 489
word is to image (in a letter) 147
words like a painters oils 381

Y

yellow blue 346
yes it fell 86

www.FrankPrem.com

www.ingramcontent.com/pod-product-compliance
Lightning Source LLC
Chambersburg PA
CBHW052039070526
44584CB00020B/3163